GW00758860

Front cover: Foggintor Quarry — Dave Brewer

The Railways, Quarries and Cottages of Foggintor

— by —
Kath Brewer

The Railways, Quarries and Cottages of Foggintor

by Kath Brewer

Copyright © Kath Brewer

ORCHARD PUBLICATIONS
2 Orchard Close, Chudleigh, Newton Abbot, Devon TQ13 0LR
Telephone: (01626) 852714

ISBN 1 898964 30 0

Typeset, Printed and Bound for Orchard Publications by
HEDGEROW PRINT
16 Marsh Lane, Lords Meadow, Crediton, Devon EX17 IES

Contents

INTRODUCTION

The reason for my love and deep interest in the Foggintor area is due to my paternal family living in the first purpose-built quarrymen's houses, Mount Pleasant (Red Cottages), and later in Hill Cottages until shortly before their demolition. My family have been in the area since the 1780s, my great x 4 grandfather Christopher Stephens (a Cornish tin miner) marrying Martha in Tavistock in 1790, their second son, Nicholas (my family), also being a miner. He and Jane his wife lived at Ball Cottage, Norsworthy Bridge, and he worked in these mines, and also (previously) at Huckworthy Bridge mine. When Nicholas died prematurely at the age of 45, Jane married John Ruby (who was born at Holne), and they moved into one of the vacant rooms at Mount Pleasant Cottages with two 'Stephens' and two 'Ruby' children – John was given as Labourer/ Granite in the 1851 Census. They lived there until the 1860s, when they moved to Gunnislake, possibly due to the quarrying slackening. This is also about the time many quarrymen emigrated to the United States of America. My Grandfather and his wife and children (including my father, who was the last of their children to be born in Cornwall) moved back about 1896 to Hill Cottages, all the sons becoming stone masons, where some stayed until Gran died in 1944, an aunt and her family then moving into that house for a few more years.

I was born at Chagford, my maternal family being tailors and there from at least the 1790s. My mother died a couple of days after my birth, so I stayed with my maternal grandmother until her death, going to my paternal grandmother at 15 months of age, and staying at Foggintor until my father re-married.

Towards the end of 1995, with our being unable to go out due to my husband Dave's continuing ill-health, he persuaded me to put all the information I had accumulated on the area into some sort of order. I started on the cottages, but had not got very far when I had a letter from Chris Stone putting forward his thoughts on the reason for the archway at Hill Cottages, together with photostats of photos he had taken at Ynys y Pandy Slate Mill, Gorseddau Quarry in Wales. His suggestion was the most sensible idea I had heard, and the similarity of the Foggintor and Welsh archways certainly seemed convincing, and the theory put forward by Chris is expounded in the Quarry section. I am most grateful to Chris, as that made me go to the West Devon Record Office again to see if there was anything relevant in the Maristow papers some now on view to the public which were not available when Dave and I went a dozen or more years ago, but I was unable to find the proof I needed.

I apologise for quoting so much from other works, but there is a sad lack of documentation for both the railways and the quarries, making it virtually impossible to double check things. People such as the Rev. Bray, give vivid descriptions of their own interpretations of what could be seen at the time. I have copied the same spelling as used in the quotes but have not put (sic) each time. It is unfortunate that years ago I did not take sufficient detail of where I obtained information. I am only too sorry we did not take more photos as a family, and also my taking for granted that things would not change, and consequently not acquiring much more information which would have helped greatly now.

For the Plymouth and Dartmoor Railway I was fortunate in having photocopies of Tyrwhitt's *Statement* and Stuart's *Prospectus* but consulted Kendall's *The Plymouth & Dartmoor Railway,* Burt's 'Notes' in Carrington's *Dartmoor, a Descriptive Poem* and Kingdom's *The Princetown Branch,* for some of the information, without which it would have been a very difficult project. I appreciate the help I received, covering quarries and quarrying, from Dr Peter Stanier for sending me photocopies of some of his own work and also other relevant papers, and Mr Chris Stone for many interesting letters in reply to some of my probably stupid questions and for drawing the various maps, etc., for me. The Cottages were easier as many of the Maristow Papers at the West Devon Record Office in Plymouth are available to the public, and I thank Elisabeth Stanbrook very much for letting me have information she came across in the Public Record Office (PRO) during her own researches.

Whilst researching, I have of course taken copies of entries for the area which covers Yes Tor/Foggintor/Red Cottages and part of Rundlestone, from the Walkhampton Census Returns between 1841 and 1891, and also from the Lydford Returns which cover the rest of the Rundlestone area.

For 'Further Reading' I have mentioned articles in various issues of *Dartmoor Magazine,* many being personal memories, as with Freddie Stoyle who lived at Walkhampton Foggintor School and Barbara Stevens who lived at Princetown and knew many of the people in the area very well. The late John Robins and Paul Rendell have both done research for their articles, as did Mavis Price whose family lived at Wheal Lucky.

I would like to also thank the following, all of whom have sent many personal letters: the late C.T. (Bud) Ambrose for information on the railway and setts; Mike Brown for items from the Maristow papers, some of which I then did not need to copy again!; Ted Fitch for finding so many sett makers bankers in the complex; Dr. Tom Greeves for the names of the stonecutters working on the corbels; the late Albert Mead, our next door neighbour for many years, for his memories; Paul Rendell for items he found at the Duchy Office, Princetown which he knew I would be interested in, and John Tonkin for his information on the Sellick involvement. The following for supplying and giving permission to use their photographs: the late E. Masson Phillips for letting me have a copy of his 1932 photo of the Manager's House, Harry Davies for the 1953 photo of Foggintor, Ron Joy for the Mission Hall, Ted Fitch, Dave German, Jenny Sanders, Elisabeth Stanbrook, Chris Stone and Stephen Woods for many photos of the area, and of course Dave, my husband for his encouragement and comments.

Kath Brewer

PART 1: THE PLYMOUTH AND DARTMOOR RAILWAYS

THE BEGINNING

The founder of Princetown, Thomas Tyrwhitt, was born on August 12th 1762 at Wickham Bishops Rectory, the son of the Rev. Edmund Tyrwhitt. He was educated at Eton and Christ Church College, Oxford, matriculating in 1780 and obtaining his B.A. and M.A. degrees. He was introduced to the Prince of Wales and became his Private Secretary and Secretary of the Prince's Council and Auditor of the Duchy of Cornwall in 1786. He was appointed Lord Warden of the Stannaries of Devon and Cornwall and also Vice Admiral of the two counties. Thomas represented Plymouth in Parliament in 1806 and became Gentleman Usher of the Black Rod in 1812 until he resigned due to ill-health in 1832. He was knighted in 1813.

In 1771 an advertisement appeared in local newspapers inviting interested people to attend a meeting at Moretonhampstead to consider making a road from there across Dartmoor to Tavistock. In about 1780 we find Mr Gullett of Prince Hall and Mr Bray of Beardon reclaiming and enclosing common land. In 1785 Tyrwhitt started enclosing, planting and laying out a farm, together with his dwelling house, Tor Royal, which were completed in 1798. The area around Princetown was open land with few trackways, so Tyrwhitt laid out and constructed roads - from Princetown to Two Bridges which no doubt included the building of Trena Bridge which was replaced by Devon County Council in 1901; to the Turnpike Road at Rundlestone, and to his house at Tor Royal. He also erected various buildings, such as the Plume of Feathers which was built in 1785 for the workmen employed in building his Tor Royal Estate and his other projects.

He was prominent in getting the prison built for the Napoleonic prisoners of war, started in 1806 and costing £127,000. When the p.o.w. prison closed in 1816, Princetown's prosperity declined - there had been a suggestion that the prison could house large numbers of orphan children (paupers) to teach them rural crafts away from the 'evil life' of London. With the abandonment of this scheme, Princetown was in danger of extinction.

Tyrwhitt thought a railroad to Plymouth would help to bring life back to Princetown and encourage agriculture on Dartmoor. He saw the completion of the railroad but was no doubt not too happy at the way things turned out, with the Johnson Brothers virtually taking over the whole concern. He died in France on 24th February 1833, aged 70, so did not see his other dream become reality – the use of the prison for convicts.

The Plymouth Breakwater was of great importance to the proposed railroad to

Princetown. Britain was virtually continuously at war between 1779 and 1815, and local defences were erected in the Plymouth area and the dockyard expanded. The Breakwater had been suggested by Admiral Lord St Vincent in 1779 when Captain of the Foudroyant, as he, Hawke, Hood and all the great admirals of the time found Cawsand Bay dangerous as an anchorage. In 1806 Thomas Tyrwhitt (for the Prince of Wales) and Admiral Sir C.M. Pole (for the Admiralty) became Members of Parliament, and in 1812 Pole helped to pass the motion in the House of Commons which granted £80,000 to start work on the Breakwater. Work commenced in 1812 when a 25 acre quarry was purchased at Pomphlett, but was not completed until 1848, at a cost of £1,000,000 with 3½ million tons of stone being used. The engineers, John Rennie and Joseph Whidbey, commenced surveying Plymouth Sound on 18th March 1806 and, when Rennie died in 1821, Whidbey continued to supervise the work at the Breakwater. In 1817 Pole was pressing the Government to speed things up to compensate for the shortage of work in the dockyard. (C. Gill, *Plymouth, A New History*). As will be seen later, the Johnson Brothers were the link between the Breakwater and the proposed railroad.

On 3rd November 1818, a *Substance of a Statement made to the Chamber of Commerce, Plymouth, concerning the Formation of a Rail Road from the Forest of Dartmoor to the Plymouth Lime-Quarries, with Additional Observations and a Plan of the Intended Line* was presented by Sir Thomas Tyrwhitt. The first two paragraphs read:

'In submitting the following thoughts to the public eye the author lays claim to no other merit than that of soliciting attention to a measure, which, founded on the basis of general, as well as local, utility, and therefore speaking for itself, required neither the embellishments of language, nor the subtleties of argument to recommend it.

To reclaim and clothe with grain and grasses a spacious tract of land, now lying barren, desolate and neglected; to fill this unoccupied region with an industrious, and hardy population; to create a profitable interchange of useful commodities between an improvable and extensive line of back country and a commercial sea-port of the first capabilities, both natural and artificial, to provide employment and subsistence for the poor of several Parishes; and to alleviate the pressure of parochial burthens, by a method, at once simply ingenious and comparatively unexpensive, form altogether such a stimulus to adventure and such a scope for exertion, especially to a wealthy Company, as must dilate the benevolent heart of the patriot, whilst it emboldens the capitalist gladly to lend his assistance in carrying the plan into execution'.
The 'Plan' further states:

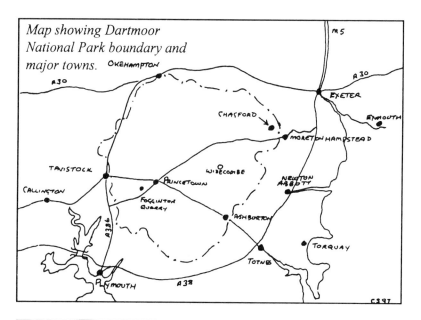

Map showing Dartmoor National Park boundary and major towns.

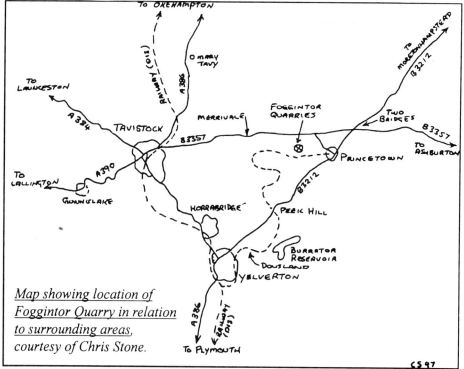

Map showing location of Fogginator Quarry in relation to surrounding areas, courtesy of Chris Stone.

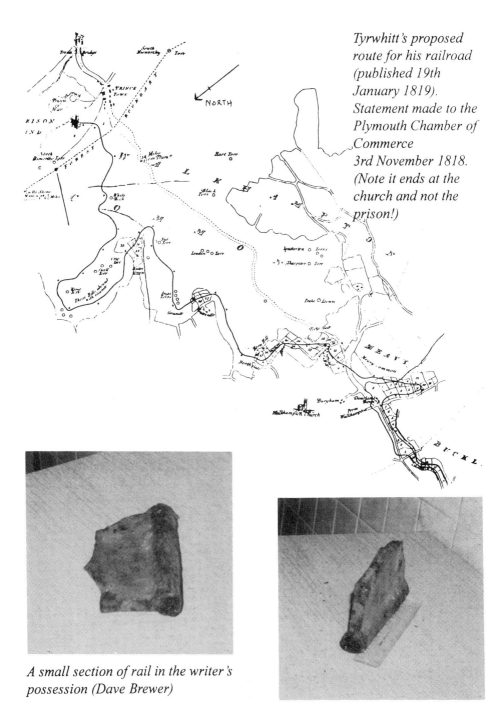

Tyrwhitt's proposed route for his railroad (published 19th January 1819). Statement made to the Plymouth Chamber of Commerce 3rd November 1818. (Note it ends at the church and not the prison!)

A small section of rail in the writer's possession (Dave Brewer)

Chair and Rail from the P. & D.R. (the late Bud Ambrose)

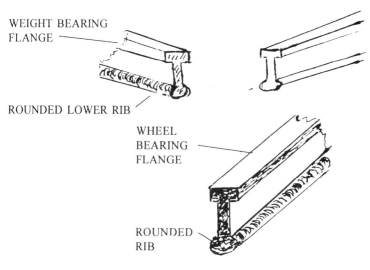

WEIGHT BEARING
FLANGE

ROUNDED LOWER RIB

WHEEL
BEARING
FLANGE

ROUNDED
RIB

'The road will commence at Dartmoor Prison, which lies about 1250 feet above the sea, and thence traverse the Moor and Roborough-Down, in a southwesterly direction, to the Laira at Crabtree, by a gradual fall of half an inch in three feet. The distance between the two places will not, in all probability exceed twenty miles, according to the line marked out in the plan; and the road ought to be an ascending and descending one, or, what is technically called, a double road.

It may be interesting to persons unacquainted with the constructive principle of rail-roads to know, that a *single* rail-road consists of an inclined plane, *nine* feet broad, bounded throughout its whole length, on each side, by grooved slips of iron, which are fitted to receive the car or waggon passing over them. The interval between the slips is composed of the same materials as a turnpike-road. A *double* road is a second road exactly similar to the first, and running parallel by its side. Both roads together occupy a breadth of *eighteen* feet.

On a descending line, a horse could readily draw to Crabtree from *twelve* to *fifteen tons* in *five* hours, and by the former, or ascending line, return to Dartmoor prison with *four tons* in *six* hours, without any of that exposure to injury and irregularity of conveyance, to which articles despatched by sea, or the usual land routes, are subject; without the least impediment from winds, rains, or frosts; and with an incalculable saving of time, expense, and animal, as well as human, labour.'

It was calculated that it would cost about £2,000 a mile. Tyrwhitt hoped to raise £45,000 by subscription in shares of £25 each, and the income would derive from the tonnage of importable and exportable commodities.

Tyrwhitt's idea was to import Lime and Sea Sand to aid the cultivation of the Moor, timber for buildings, coal for heating, culm, groceries and furniture. He also expected trees to be planted, 'stone easter pine, Scotch fir, larch and other hardy trees' for sale later. The exportable commodities would be Granite, Peat, Mining Products ('If iron, copper and tin could be raised and smelted on the spot without the necessity of resorting elsewhere, the saving of expense, both to government and the public, might be decidedly pronounced as incalculable'), Flax, Hemp, and possibly even rape, cabbages and turnips. Travelling Vehicles and Parcels were another consideration:

'The busy operations of agriculture and other concerns will be continually impelling the numerous persons engaged in them in various directions up and down the line of the road, to whom a car, drawn by one horse, must offer itself as a great convenience. From the peculiar construction of the road, the horse will be able to travel with ease at the rate of seven miles per hour, drawing a load in proportion.'

Tyrwhitt also refers to the TRANSFER OF CONVICTS TO DARTMOOR PRISON as follows:

'In case government should resolve on the removal of the convicts to Dartmoor, a farther traffic on the road, occasioned by the supply of their various necessities, will become certain, whether this supply is contracted for in the port of Plymouth or a more distant quarter.

The perfect state of repair, in which the prison buildings are kept, might justify the inference, that they will not long remain without inhabitants. The author, however, abstains from entering into particulars on this point, while the removal, above referred to, continues doubtful. *

* The author is happily enabled to quote here an interesting extract from the printed *Report by a Committee of the House of Commons on the Prisons of the Metropolis, concerning Dartmoor Prison*, which, if it had been expressly written for the present pamphlet, could not be more apposite:–

'Your Committee have received in evidence, that the forest of Dartmoor contains about 130,000 acres of land; one-fifth of which is inclosed; that a considerable part is the property of His Royal Highness the Prince Regent, as Duke of Cornwall; that the prison thereon has formerly contained from 8,000 to 9,000 prisoners of war; and that 2,000 convicts may be well secured there, with proper divisions for classification and work rooms. It appears, by professional evidence laid before your Committee, that the situation of the prison on Dartmoor is indisputably healthy; that provisions are cheap; that fuel is to be acquired for the labour only; and that the utmost expenses for the proposed alterations of the prison would not exceed £5,000. It is evident to your Committee, that the proposed conversion of Dartmoor Prison into a prison for convicts would place it in a more perfect state for a prison of war at any future period, as your Committee have received in evidence, that, if it remains unoccupied, it must inevitably fall into decay. Your Committee, therefore, beg leave to direct the attention of His Majesty's Government to this subject, for the prisoners might be speedily removed from the contagious vices of the metropolis, wherein the completion of one crime is mostly the precursor of another more iniquitous, and the youthful delinquent, by compulsatory labour, in the first instance, would be withdrawn from those habits of idleness, which never fail to engender depravity and to afford an opportunity for the imitation of bad example.

By such regulations, it appears to your Committee, that the means of actual subsistence would be acquired by the convicts themselves, therein affording an incitement to labour and consequently an urgent inclination for a return to virtuous habits. Dartmoor abounds with *granite* of an excellent quality, well adapted for the purpose of building or paving; and as His Majesty's Government are at this time purchasing large quantities for various public works, your Committee conceive, that convicts would be capable of cutting granite to any extent for such purposes, and that such a process would cleanse the land and render it fit for cultivation. Turf also may be cut to any quantity, and a canal, or *iron rail way,* might convey it to Plymouth. There are also great falls of water in every part of the Moor, and your Committee are of opinion, that *cloth* might be manufactured by the prisoners for their own clothing, as large quantities of coarse wool can be obtained upon the spot... The House will observe, that, in the judgment of several respectable witnesses, great advantages may be derived from the application of the labour of convicts at Dartmoor. On this your Committee refrain from expressing any opinion: but they think it proper to direct the attention of the House to the evidence in the Minutes on that subject.'

The original survey of the Plymouth and Dartmoor Rail-Road was undertaken by William Shillibeer, a schoolmaster at Walkhampton and a part-time surveyor on Sir Masseh Lopes' estate. The verbal prospectus given to the Plymouth Chamber of Commerce was followed on 30th November 1818 by the depositing of Shillibeer's plans with the Clerk of the Peace at Exeter to enable a Bill to be placed before the next session of Parliament. William Stuart, Rennie's engineer in charge of the Breakwater works, had been 'borrowed' by Sir Thomas from the Admiralty on a part-time basis to supervise the railroad and on 8th January 1819, the following Prospectus appeared under his name:

PROSPECTUS OF THE PLYMOUTH AND DARTMOOR RAIL-ROAD

'The Survey of this undertaking, as now finally terminated, is, on every consideration, perfectly satisfactory: and what by many at the commencement was thought quite impracticable, has been accomplished, by a fall of only half an inch in three feet, upon a distance not exceeding twenty-two miles, commencing at the Prison of War on the Forest of Dartmoor, and concluding at Plymouth Harbour and Lime Rocks.

Perhaps no measure of this magnitude was ever offered to public notice, in which there have incurred fewer difficulties. There are no buildings to be demolished no intrusion to be made upon any property, where the land can be said to be of any great value; no machinery is requisite in any part of the line, nor are any bridges necessary to be built.

No person, who is at all acquainted with the district through which the line of road will pass, can for a moment doubt the immense advantages that will result to it from the measure proposed.

It is therefore needless to make further comments on this head; and I shall now proceed to state the profits likely to arise from the traffic of the Rail-Road, and which, in my opinion, fully justify the expence to be incurred. I would then take as

Exports		Tons	s.d.	£. s. d
Granite		4000	5.0.	1000. 0.0.

Upon this article I speak with more precision, perhaps, than any other, having surveyed the whole of the Torrs, the quality of the Stone is excellent; and there are going round to the Navy Board, *at their own special request,* some specimens which I will venture to say can scarcely be surpassed in any other quarter; as to quantity, the Company will be enabled to enter upon any Contract, however extensive.

		Tons	s.d.	£. s. d
Agricultural Productions		1000	2.6	125. 0.0
Turf, per load, by one Horse		100	2.6	12.10.0
Market Cars	2 No. £20 per Year each			40. 0.0
Rubble Granite for House Building		2000	1.0	100. 0.0
Ditto for Causeways		1000	1.6	75. 0.0
Small Stones and Gravel for Roads		1500	1.0	75. 0.0

Imports				
Coals and Kennel *		680	6.0	204. 0.0
Culm		768	2.6	96. 0.0
Lime		2500	2.6	312.10.0
Mud from Sutton Pool and Plymouth Harbour		1000	2.6	125. 0.0
Sea Sand		1000	2.6	125. 0.0
Building Materials		2000	6.0	600. 0.0
Market Cars	2 No. £20 per Year			40. 0.0
Total of Exports and Imports				£2930. 0.0

With these calculations, which are taken at a lower rate than is usual on such occasions, and after the maturest deliberation, I, with confidence, leave the undertaking to the countenance and patronage of those who have capital to invest; requesting them always to bear in mind one peculiar benefit which the project offers, among many others, viz. that no re-shipment will be necessary of any article exported.

The estimate of the whole expence, in which I have included every call that will be made for the execution of the plan, will not exceed the sum of £45,000, to be raised in Shares of £25 each.

(Signed) W. Stuart.
(Manager of the Quarries for the Plymouth Breakwater).
* Subscriptions will be received at all the Banks in Plymouth, Dock, and Exeter, and by most of the Bankers in London.
Plymouth, January 8th, 1819'.

As one can see from the fore-going, it was to be a very busy, money-making line! The First Meeting of the subscribers was held at the Guildhall, Plymouth, on 24th March 1819, when a provisional Committee of seven was elected, Sir Thomas not being among them.

At a meeting on 20th May, Tyrwhitt became one of the committee members and invested over £3,000 of his own money in the scheme. Sir Masseh Lopes was the next largest investor. The Company agreed to apply to the Exchequer Loans Commission for £10,000 to avoid more than 20% calls on the subscribers annually. The Act became law on 2nd July 1819, authorising the Plymouth and Dartmoor Rail-Road Company to construct a line of about 24 miles in length from Crabtree Inn, Laira, via Jump on to Leigham, Fursdon, Clearbrook, Yelverton Down, Dousland, Yennadon Down to Peek Hill, Ingra Tor, circumnavigating Swell Tor and King Tor and finally to Princetown. At a Meeting on 8th June 1819, Mr Stuart, the Surveyor, proposed that the rail-road could be built as a single iron railway without detriment to any of the prospective benefits, and the expense should not exceed £27,783, which figure included the purchase of necessary land.

Also in July 1819, Sir Masseh Lopes was asked a price for granite from Walkhampton Common. He later offered unlimited granite from the Common at a Royalty of 2d per ton. The Company decided that they had no authority to go into business as stone merchants and the acting committee was instructed to find

* Kennel/Cannel-Coal: a bituminous coal that burns with a bright flame, and is much used for making coal oils and gas.

a private firm to work in liaison with the Company, Sir Thomas and Edmund Lockyer being appointed as Trustees regarding a lease for the granite.

The First General Meeting of the Proprietors was held on 20th September 1819, and a Managing Committee was elected - Sir Wm. Elford, Bart., Treasurer; W. Burt, Secretary to the Chamber of Commerce, Plymouth, Clerk; G.D. Wood, Collector; Wm. Stuart, Superintendent of the Plymouth Breakwater Works, Engineer; Hugh MacIntosh of London, Contractor for forming the road; and Bailey and Co. of London, Contractors for supplying the iron.

On 3rd July 1820, another Act was passed authorising a further £7,200 to cover the necessary extension to Sutton Pool, following which exactly a year later an additional sum of £5,000 was required to re-align part of the track to eliminate a too severe gradient between Jump and Leigham Mill, and also for excavating the tunnel at Leigham.

On 12th August 1819, Sir Thomas laid the first rail at Laira. They were of parabolic edge-rail type, butt-jointed within the chairs and only some 2 feet 10 inches in length. The depth varied from 4 inches at the ends to 6 inches at mid point, and the gauge was 4 feet 6 inches. Tenders were invited for the section between Jump and Princetown by the 30th May 1820. The first course of metal or stone was to be 12 feet wide and 9 inches thick, except where the turn-out or passing places (two in each mile) were, when it should be 24 feet in width. This was to be laid two months before the stone blocks and rails were to be fixed, when a second course of metal or small broken stone was to be laid, 9 inches thick and 24 feet wide, and covered with 3 feet of gravel. Also there were to be fences 28 feet in width. The Contractor was to keep it repaired for twelve months after completion; replace any broken rails, but could use the rails until the road was completed when he had to make good any damage which had occurred.

(Kendall)

THE JOHNSON INVOLVEMENT

By 1819 William Johnson, a Londoner, with his partner Brice, became involved. According to Kendall, in the early part of the nineteenth century, Johnson had an interest in Hay Tor granite on the other side of the Moor, whose high quality granite had secured the Breakwater contract for him. The partners approached the Plymouth and Dartmoor Company with a proposition, as they not only required stone for the Breakwater works, but also had in mind paving stones in Plymouth, Stonehouse and Dock, and building the new baths in Plymouth. They offered a flat rate of 2/6d per ton, subject to an average of 8000 tons per annum for seven years for the carriage of granite, irrespective of distance. This should have provided a steady income of £1,000 per annum to the rail road. An agreement was signed on the 21st September 1820, and Johnson and Brice were granted a long lease for the granite on Walkhampton Common from Sir Masseh Lopes. However, the following information was found by Elisabeth Stanbrook in the Minute Book at the Public Record Office:

21.9.1820. The Plymouth & Dartmoor Railway Co. discussed granting Johnson & Brice an Under Lease for the quarries on Walkhampton Common.

7.2.1821. The P&DR Co. granted the Under Lease to Johnson & Brice

12.3.1821. The Under Lease was confirmed at a Special General Assembly of the P&DR Co.

A Mr Roger Hopkins replaced Mr Stuart as Engineer, and in 1821 designed a new type of rail, being lap-jointed instead of butt-jointed.

The Committee could not meet their first capital repayment of the Exchequer Loan, and MacIntosh was also requesting payment for his work. At a General Meeting on 29th June 1822, Johnson Brothers were to become the contractors in place of MacIntosh. The Company were still in financial difficulties, and on 18th May 1823 the Exchequer Loans Committee agreed to advance another £10,000, but only against personal sureties as well as those of the Company, and on 11th August 1823 a further Deed of Mortgage was executed with the Company, backed by Sir Masseh Lopes, Sir Wm. Elford, Sir Hy. Sawyer, Sir Thomas Tyrwhitt and John Johnson Jnr.

On 26th September 1823, the completed line from King Tor to Sutton Pool, which was transporting lime, coals, timber and other articles one way, and granite and various other items the other, was opened by Sir Thomas Tyrwhitt at his Wharf on Roborough Down, with festivities and a Breakfast for about a thousand people. Brooking Rowe in TDA 1905 quotes from a newspaper dated 2nd October

1823, that after the breakfast 'a long file of cars, partly laden with granite and partly with the stewards and other individuals, accompanied by the band and ornamented with flags, set off for Plymouth, where they were heartily greeted by the huzzas of a large concourse of people. Fifty gentlemen afterwards dined at the Royal Hotel'.

However, Kendall says Humphrey Woollcombe wrote in his diary what actually happened:

'On Friday the 26th September, the Railroad was opened. We were invited to a public breakfast by Sir Thomas Tyrwhitt at a place called by him North Wharf near Elfordtown where marquees were erected and a breakfast laid out in a large building. Unfortunately about twelve rain came in and dispersed most of the ladies. I got into a car and went in the procession but unfortunately there was no arrangement and everything fell into confusion and consequently compleat order could never be re-established nor preserved, had it been the scene would have been a very pleasing one.

The stoppages in waiting for other cars to come up made us lose two hours and we did not reach Plymouth until seven o'clock, rather too long to be shut up in vehicles without anything to eat or drink. The scenery for a part of the way is very beautiful, particularly from Marsh House to Fancy on the bank of the Plym.'

Burt's comments, which appeared in a newspaper of the time, summed up his feelings:

'Language is incompetent to describe the grandeur and beauty of the scenery through which the railway passes. But the beauties of nature, however impressive, are secondary to the higher objects which arise to the minds eye in traversing such scenes. The merchant and the trader, the manufacturer and the agriculturist, must all fondly, and not without hope, look to the period, when, by their combined endeavours, the railway will be devoted to busy traffic, and a population shall arise to consume the importations, and to furnish the exports through various channels of commerce. Dartmoor, so long condemned to sterility, in a few years may again wear the verdure of woods, and corn, and grass, and no longer stand as a bye word and a reproach for its infertility, in other counties. To Sir Thomas Tyrwhitt the measure is indebted for its origin; and the spirited proprietors, assisted by their committees, chairmen, contractors and engineers, have succeeded in defiance of all obstacles, in achieving a task which reflects credit, not only on them collectively, nay, on the whole of the country.'

Front view of Wharf on Roborough Down *(Elisabeth Stanbrook)*

Rear view of Wharf on Roborough Down *(Elisabeth Stanbrook)*

The Dartmoor Tramroad at Laira　　　　　　*(Dave German Collection)*

*The 12th milestone on
Roborough Down
(Dave Brewer)*

Brooking Rowe passed further comments on the Wharf, as follows:

'The Wharf on Roborough Down reminds me of another useful enterprise of Tyrwhitts. It was a large building, which he had had erected as a depot for the reception and distribution of various necessaries; an establishment which proved most useful to farmers in the neighbourhood, who were able to obtain lime, seeds, potatoes and other farming requirements from thence at moderate prices and a saving of carriage. He had a similar building at Princetown near the terminus of the railway'

Possibly this refers to the building at the Wharf, and the one in Princetown would not have been used until after the completion of the railroad in 1826.

The promoters obviously envisaged a busy line, even with other owners using the line provided they put their name on the outside of their wagons. There were also tolls for carrying horses, cattle, pigs and sheep.

On the 6th July 1824, Roger Hopkins had to appear before the Quarter Sessions at Exeter to obtain the necessary Certificate for the opened part of the line. The contractors were instructed to place mile stones beside the line. Some are still in existence today. They are of granite, cylindrical in shape with the top set at an angle and with the mileage shown from Sutton.

In return for completing the railway from King Tor to Princetown at their own expense, and which was opened in December 1826 (the final cost being 'about £66,000'), the Johnson Brothers were given a mortgage on the line. As they also worked the quarries, they were enabled to pay mortgage interest offset against the tolls they owed – in other words, they virtually had the monopoly and free transport for their granite.

The Committee negotiated an agreement in 1827 whereby Johnsons agreed to relinquish their monopoly in 1834 for a rate reduction to 1s. 10d per ton instead of the previous 2s. 6d. The Exchequer Loans Commission were not too happy about this, as they had received no returns for the previous three years. In 1828 an arbitrator had assessed the company's debt to Johnson as being over £24,000.

In 1829 a short branch to the Cann Quarry joined the railway near Plym Bridge – this was to transport the good quality blue slate stone which was in high demand; in 1833 a branch was built by John and William Johnson for Lord Morley from Marsh Mills to Plympton to move the china clay.

During 1830, the Rev. Bray of Tavistock had 'entered upon the rail-road at Roborough Down, and pursued it till I came opposite Walkhampton, when I was obliged to return to Tavistock' and in May 1831 he 'mounted my horse to resume my exploration'. He approaches a tor, probably between Yes Tor and Swell Tor, and says:

'the railroad for once assumes a picturesque appearance where it takes a sudden turn at the base of a lofty rock, which seemed, notwithstanding, almost a 'baseless fabric' as the light was visible through an aperture between the smaller stones on which it was up-piled. The hills in the distance formed for it a good background. Some huts, one a blacksmith's shop, now presented themselves. And before it stood a vehicle, not much unlike a rude kind of vis-a-vis, with an awning. This I had observed passing on with some degree of rapidity before us. I conclude that in these carriages with iron wheels, though as cumbrous and perhaps uneasy as the scythed cars of the Britons, many pleasure-parties make excursions from Plymouth, for a man accosted me, and said that if I wished to see the works, Mr Johnson or Thompson, or a person of some such name, would show them to me.'

1835 found the Plymouth and Dartmoor Railway with its completed main line, branches to Sutton Pool and Plympton and a private branch to Cann Quarry. There was heavy traffic in granite, and growing amounts of slate stone and china clay, which should have made a flourishing company. Unfortunately, the Contractors, (Johnsons), were owed £28,000 and £18,000 was still owed to the Exchequer Loans Committee (the second £10,000 had reluctantly been paid by the 'personal' signatories from their own money), and threats were made to take assets to defray the public debt. It would appear that the Johnsons around this period paid the Exchequer debt in order to save the railway, enabling them to continue in business.

Nathaniel Beardmore, under the supervision of James M. Rendel, surveyed a line to be known as the 'Plymouth and Devonport to Exeter Railway over Dartmoor with a branch to Tavistock'. The plans were deposited at the office of the Clerk of the Peace for Devon on 29th February 1840, and Kingdom mentions a report which appeared in the Plymouth and Devonport Weekly Journal of 29th October 1840, and included the following:

'The line was to commence at Pennycomequick – a suburb of Plymouth, and be carried by way of the Houndiscombe Valley across the Devonport road to Manadon, thence to Jump, to the valley of the Plym, thence through Meavy to Sheepstor bridge, and so enter Dartmoor, on to Siwards or Nun's Cross. Over Dartmoor, the line passes Whiteworks Mine, down the valley of the Swincombe river, across the West Dart river, and through Prince Hall Estate, into the Cherrybrook valley at the bridge on the Tavistock to Moreton road - then down the valley which runs parallel with the road to the nearby Postbridge, where it crosses the East Dart river, and sweeping around to the south of the Merripit Estate, enters the Runnage valley, near the farmhouse of that name, and passing up the valley, leaves Dartmoor by the New House Pass, near Vitifer Mine.'

Leaving the high ground, it went to Chagford Bridge, followed the Teign to Fingle and Clifford Bridges, on to Dunsford, and so to Exeter.

There was talk of dams being placed on the Blackabrook and Cowsic to work two water wheels to haul the trains up from Meavy to Nuns Cross, and another north of Postbridge on the East Dart to haul trains from Chagford to Newhouse (Newhouse was opposite where the Warren House Inn now stands). There would also have been tunnels near Newhouse and Nuns Cross, and the Plymouth and Dartmoor Railroad shareholders hoped that this possible beginning of railway communication throughout the country would help their company. Fortunately, this railway never materialised.

Plans for a railway from Exeter to Plymouth had been deposited by the South Devon Company in November 1843. The Plymouth and Dartmoor Company received a draft of the South Devon Bill in April, and there were no provisions for the P. & D. to provide facilities for the South Devon Company, as Marsh Mills and Laira were common to them both. At the P.& D. Meeting on January 2nd 1844, the Committee decided to write to the Exchequer Loans Committee asking why their demands concerning the £18,000 loan had ceased, having received no correspondence since 1835, to which they received no reply. It nevertheless came as a shock when a reprint of the South Devon Bill was received by them in May, and the opening phrases were: *'And whereas Messrs John and William Johnson are in possession of and claim to be entitled as mortgagees or assignees to the said Plymouth and Dartmoor Railway, or the Rates, Tolls and Duties arising thereon'* (Kendall). Not only had the railway faded financially in the 1830s, when presumably a lesser number of items other than granite and the Cann Quarry slate stone were transported, but now the proprietors were not going to reap any benefit through the Johnsons unknown intervention.

There had to be negotiations between the Johnsons and the South Devon due to the necessary crossing of the P.& D.R. at Laira, and terms were eventually agreed. On 23rd April 1851 the South Devon agreed to pay £13,000 for a portion of the Plymouth and Dartmoor Railroad between the Rising Sun Inn and Sutton Pool, and to have both gauges on this stretch so that the P.& D. wagons would still reach the harbour. In 1852 the South Devon bought some of the Cann Railway from Lord Morley, and agreed to build a branch line to Lee Moor.

In May 1865 the Plymouth and Dartmoor Committee approved a Bill to be presented to Parliament for the reconstruction of the Company, By this time, apart from Johnson, there were none of the original Committee Members left.

The Company was to create £75,000 of Preference Shares, which Debentures were all to be in the name of William Johnson, which represented in effect the purchase price of the line by the new Company. Johnson later transferred all his shares to Ben and Walter Bovill, the latter becoming Chairman of the Railway, which marked the end of Johnsons' connections with the railroad, and as Crossing in his *Dartmoor Worker* wrote:

'The tramway and the quarries were in the hands of one company, and the former continued in regular use until 1865, granite being daily despatched to the Cattewater. In that year the line was acquired by another company, who held it until about 1879, when the portion of it extending from the eastern verge of Roborough Down to its termination at Princetown, was purchased by the Princetown Railway Co. who constructed their line upon it throughout the greater part of its course. Sidings were formed at the quarries, and the granite has since been conveyed over it.'

In the Maristow papers there were comments on the Johnsons and the railroad – to start with there are a few presentments:

1796   Mr Tyrwhitt for Inclosing a part of Walkhampton Common
1820   The person or persons for cutting a road through different parts of Sir Masseh Lopes Lands
1821   The Trustees of the New Rail Road for making several dangerous pits in different places at Yennadown and Dartmore Common
1826   The Proprietors of the Dartmore Railway for blocking up a Foot Path leading from Croftshead to Church Lane
1829   The P.& D.R. for not keeping their Fences and Drains in repair
1841   John Johnson Esqur. for a Quary at Swell Tor not in work near Easter Green being very dangeorus
1845   The Dartmoor Railway Co. for not filling with stones the hollow between their Rails where their road crosses the Parish Road at the foot of Little Yennadon whereby the Crossing is rendered dangerous with Wheel Carriage.

There were also three or four further complaints similar to the 1841 one above, regarding 'leaving open Dangerous Quarries on Walkhampton Commons at Ingetor, Incline Plane and Swell Tor at present not in working'.

The Estate Letter Book contains letters written by Geo. Giles, who ran the Estate, to either Johnson or Filmer who dealt with matters for the Johnsons, and the contents were mentioned to Sir Ralph Lopes. Many concerned repairs to gates, gaps in walls, etc. along the railroad; alterations near Prince Rock where the boundary needed fixing and setting; rents being over-due, also tithes due to Rev.

Geo. Richards and Rev. Amos Crymes. In a letter to Johnson in April 1833, Giles mentions that the late Sir Masseh and Sir Ralph's claim for the use of the Quay at Prince Rock had never been settled, and he trusted Johnson would now be ready to meet 'this affair'. On 20th September 1833 the North Devon Wharf was being conveyed to Sir Ralph, who wished to 'dispose of it at rent' and it was offered to Johnson. In March 1838 800 Bushels of Lime was ordered from Filmer to be delivered to Jump, but on 19th April a complaint was sent asking for it to be taken back and replaced due to it being very bad with too many ashes. A letter to Filmer on 11th October 1839 stated:

'Unwarranted liberties with the Farmers Help Rail Road Wagon, during the last year or two, with people not being honest enough to render an account of the use made of it. Arrears are wanted for its hiring, Toll Books could assist from 1st January 1838 to Lady Day 1839 when the Wagon broke down.'

It would be nice to know the outcome of some of these matters!

THE GREAT WESTERN RAILWAY

The new Plymouth and Dartmoor Railway Company was getting reasonable tolls from granite and china clay, and in 1873/74 purchased 600 tons of rails to put the line in good order. There was even a dividend declared – the first ever – but only 5 shillings per £100.

According to Kendall, there are no examples of the P.& D. rolling stock surviving, although a couple of perfect examples of the original parabolic edge-rails were uncovered by the G.W.R. during relaying operations at Swell Tor at the turn of the century. These were preserved by the G.W.R. and were in the Clapham Transport Museum but were probably transferred to the National Railway Museum, York.

In 1874, plans were deposited with the Clerk of the Peace for Devon for railway lines to Princetown. Under pressure from the Government the G.W.R. agreed the purchase of the Plymouth and Dartmoor route from Yelverton to Princetown in 1877. The Bill was presented, and became law on 13th August 1878, and five years later, an agreement was reached between the Plymouth and Dartmoor Company and the Great Western Railway that the latter company should not only work the line but also have controlling interest in it. The line was opened on 11th August 1883 with very scant celebrations.

Not many years after the G. W. R. railway was opened, there was a terrible blizzard. On 9th March 1891 two women and four male passengers were marooned when the train became stuck in a huge snowdrift at Eggworthy Cutting. They were trapped for 48 hours, but on the second morning, they attracted a farmer, who took them to his farm. The train was not dug out until 17th March. There were, of course, many more problems over the years, such as at the end of 1927, when the smaller quarry at Foggintor was completely filled with snow, and in 1947, the worst weather since 1891, when naval personnel from Devonport were made available to dig the train out, and in 1963. It was more than likely that every winter the trains would get into some difficulties due to ice rather more than with snow.

In the early days there were just two stations on the line, at Princetown and Dousland, or Dowsland Barn as it was then called. Passengers had to alight and embark at Horrabridge for this line, a station not being constructed at Yelverton until 1885. Due to the reduction of freight from the quarries, and to encourage visitors to the area, Burrator and Sheepstor Halt was opened in 1924, King Tor Halt on 2nd March 1928, with Ingra Tor Halt following on 2nd March 1936. Ingra Tor had their famous G.W.R. notice that, *'IN THE INTERESTS OF GAME*

PRESERVATION AND FOR THEIR PROTECTION AGAINST SNAKES, ETC.
DOGS SHOULD BE KEPT ON A LEAD. BY ORDER'

William Duke, who was born in Jersey, was the Manager of the Granite Works at Foggintor on the 1871 Census Return. However, in 1876 he opened the quarry at Merrivale, and his business expanded. The main problem was the transportation of his granite, it having to go by road to Tavistock, as there was no rail line nearby. John Somers Cocks wrote in *Devon & Cornwall Notes & Queries* of 1971 that:

'In 1908 Dukes applied for a Light Railway Order to connect them to the Princetown line, but though sanctioned, the work was never carried out.'

This railway was to branch off the main track more or less where the Swell Tor Siding started, it would pass Little King Tor, sweep around and cross the Longash Brook on a large bridge, making another sweep around Longash Hill, through a cutting, crossing the Two Bridges to Tavistock Road on a bridge, crossing the River Walkham on another embankment, and then to the Quarry, where an embankment had actually been started. It is fortunate this was never built, although it would have been an easier way for the Merrivale Quarry granite to be transported than by road. On a visit to Merrivale Quarry in July 1992, a lorry was seen removing stone from the latter embankment, for use in sea defences in Cornwall.

The Princetown Railway finally closed in March 1956, which was a great blow to all us passengers who loved travelling on it, due mainly to the increasing cost of operation and ever increasing competition from coaches and cars. In 1956 it was hoped funds could be raised to purchase the line and run it as a private venture, but the response was insignificant.

The following quotes are from many cuttings in a scrap book we had the pleasure of reading many years ago, but unfortunately the original sources are unknown, although they are probably from one of the 'local' papers:

'13th February 1956.

In the office of British Railways district engineer in Plymouth hangs the photograph of a predecessor who was largely responsible for the planning and construction of the Princetown branch line.

Now it will probably fall to Mr N.A. Cox, the present district engineer, to take up the 10½ miles of permanent way, remove the signalling and locomotive shed gear, salvage the metal bridges, and recover anything else of value.

The little wooden halts at Burrator, Ingra Tor and King Tor will be dismantled, the naked, scarred track, winding its way across the Moor, will

Magpie Viaduct, Horrabridge (Brewer Collection)

Yelverton Station (Brewer Collection)

Burrator Halt (Brewer Collection)

The 'Princetown Express' (Brewer Collection)

On the Railway near Ingra Tor   *(Brewer Collection)*

King Tor Halt   *(Brewer Collection)*

Yes Tor Brook Bridge, P. & D.R. Railway   *(Elisabeth Stanbrook)*

Bridge on G.W.R. near Ingra Tor, after repair by the D.N.P.A.

(Elisabeth Stanbrook)

Approaching Princetown   *(Brewer Collection)*

Princetown Station   *(Brewer Collection)*

Princetown Station   *(Brewer Collection)*

Entering the Station   *(Brewer Collection)*

The Crossing Gate from Dousland now in Princetown   *(Dave Brewer)*

Removing the G.W.R. Rails
(Brewer Collection)

remain for a time as a memorial of a public service which lasted 73 years, and was killed by economics.

The branch line dies on March 5th. Dismemberment of its physical equipment will take about three months from start to finish.

A new method of rail recovery will speed the process. Formerly one section of line at a time was dismantled and carried by men to the truck. The new way is to pull up three or four lengths at a time with a locomotive and draw them along the track on wheels to a loading point.

The line will yield a large quantity of steel and cast iron – most of the curves, because of their sharpness, are filled with a third rail. The Princetown station building may be let for other purposes and British Railways would be interested in offers for the track.

Stretches of other closed lines have been merged in this way into adjoining land. But while it remains railway property, the Princetown route will have to be kept fenced.

The district engineer responsible for the branch was Mr T.H. Gibbons (1891-1908) but he did the work while holding the appointment of assistant – the line was opened in 1883.'

'3rd March 1956.

Last Day of Princetown Railway. Station already wearing a derelict look.

Although the last train does not steam in until tonight Princetown Station already wears a look of decay. Its windows are boarded up and most of the equipment has been taken away. When the final train has been dealt with the staff will pack up their belongings and go quietly home. They do not want a 'line-closing ceremony'.

All of the men have been offered new appointments within the Plymouth area. But for most of them it means a search for new homes and the severing of long-established ties.

This week has been an ironic one for the men. The line is being closed because it does not pay, yet traffic during the past few days has been the heaviest experienced for a long time.

Hundreds of people, including school parties and the staff of a Plymouth store, have taken a last ride along the 10½ miles of Moorland track. Instead of the normal single coach, three coaches have been required. Although scores of inquiries have been made about the time of the last train, the Princetown Stationmaster, Mr W.G. West, did not anticipate exceptionally heavy traffic because so many people have travelled during the week.

The last train from Princetown to Yelverton is at 6.10p.m. today. There will be another normal service train from Yelverton to Princetown at 7 p.m. but this will not return to Yelverton with normal traffic.

The closure of the line has meant a tremendous amount of clerical work at the tiny station, and extra staff has been assigned to stock-take and clear things up. At the same time, workmen have torn down partitions and fences to provide wood for boarding up the windows. The job of locking up and ending the line's 73 years of life will fall to Mr West. After 18 months at the station he is being transferred to Tavistock Junction Marsh Mills, Plymouth.

One of the most reluctant to see the line close is Mr Gilbert Hext, of New Station Cottages, Princetown, who completed 41 years as a ganger on the line on Thursday. He is the longest serving man on the branch.

He recalls two occasions – during the winters of 1915 and 1947 – when the line was blocked by snow for three days.

Together with several of his workmates, Mr Hext is being transferred to Tavistock. 'I should have liked to stay on and finish my time here' he said.

Mr Bill Gough, who has spent 21 years driving between Yelverton and Princetown will drive the last train. His home is at New Station Cottages, a few yards from the station. 'Its going to be a big break' he said, 'I don't want to go. I was happy here. Still, we've got to look these things in the face. You can't run lines at a loss'. His view was shared by Mr Cyril Stephens, of Princetown, who has fired for Mr Gough for the past eight years.

Mr Stephens added 'The worst thing about it is that we've all got to find new homes, and that's no joke these days',

Mr Gough and Mr Stephens, together with the remaining crew, driver Fred Cole of Bittaford, and Fireman Ron Hext of Princetown, will be transferred to Laira, Plymouth. Watching the crowds of people milling about the station platform after the arrival of one of the trains, one of the railway staff observed 'If only they had always used it so frequently we should never have been closed down'.

T.W.E. Roche made a few interesting observations in his *Go Great Western*:

'The Commission acted with great speed; a contractor's engine was at work lifting during most of 1957 and by the end of the year the track, signalling and level crossing gates had gone. Some odd things remained: the station nameboard at Princetown, where the station was almost intact; the wire fences surrounding the moorland route; most of the wooden platform at Ingra Tor, the lamp leaning drunkenly, the 'snake' notice with its wording getting fainter and fainter. King Tor Halt was completely removed, only the pile of ash which formed the base of the platform being visible to the discerning eye. Burrator likewise disappeared save for the stone base of the platform and, oddly enough, the iron swing gate leading down to the Dam. Dousland was left a mess; the ground frame box, its equipment ripped out, suffered from much broken glass. A coal factor took over the goods yard and built an enclosure across the site of the track; the station building alone looked neat, converted into a trim bungalow.'

And finally, a quote from *Princetown Railways* by Colin Henry Bastin:

'(After Closure)

After the lines closure rumours about it's being reopened abounded, yet never really got a chance to come into hard facts, or even get off the ground, because of British Railways hasty decision to dismantle the lines tracks. Which many local people blamed on pressure coming on BR from Dartmoor National Park, whose members said in no uncertain terms 'that the old railway was nothing more than a decaying eyesore on the beauty of the moor where it ran and should be removed as soon as possible'. What was so strange about such comments from this body was that the National Park members had fought long and hard before the lines closure to keep the same railway branch in being, which they now wanted removed at all costs. I've been told privately by former BR officials, that in fact, if someone had come in quick with cash in their hands, the line between Dousland and Princetown, as it stood, could have been theirs for the sum of around £25,000.'

Through pressure again by the Dartmoor National Park Authority and the Dartmoor Preservation Association, Princetown station was removed in the summer of 1960, and all that remained were the ' Private Road/Path' signs at the ends of the access points to the site, In the last few years, the National Park have made a path suitable for wheelchairs and pushchairs from the car park, with the site of the station on one side and the wet ground of Meavy Head on the other. The old railway line to Peek Hill is now a cycle track.

In 1964, Devon County Council called for the demolition of the bridge over the Yelverton to Princetown road at Peek Hill – Prison warders would often be posted there during a jailbreak. The road was then later widened there, and it took 2½ hours on Sunday May 31st to demolish the bridge, and later 1150 tons of debris were transported to fill in Devils Elbow, three miles away towards Princetown when the alignment was to be altered for safety reasons.

In 1994 the last remaining building at Princetown Station, the station stables, were to be repaired, and the Duchy of Cornwall were to grant a lease on the property to the Dartmoor National Park Authority. The station building at Dousland survives and is now a private bungalow, backing on to the Yelverton/Princetown road near the crossroads.

Hemery in his *Walking the Dartmoor Railroads* says that rails were removed from many stretches of the Plymouth and Dartmoor Railroad line in 1916 to be melted down for munitions manufacture. There is not much to be seen of the remains of either railway now – at Yes Tor Bottom the P. & D.R. and G.W.R. lines differed – the P.& D.R. can be seen making a loop to the east, whereas the G.W.R. was able to make a tighter curve; also at Little King Tor the lines took slightly different routes, both of which can be clearly seen. Tyrwhitt's Wharf is still intact by the Yelverton Golf Course, and setts can still be seen around the roundabout at Yelverton.

Thus another episode in the history of Dartmoor ended after 133 years.

PART 2: THE QUARRIES

Geologists date the arrival of Dartmoor Granite to about 290 million years ago, and of course a band of it goes down through Cornwall over Bodmin Moor to the Scilly Isles and further out to sea. The first known people to live permanently on Dartmoor around 4,000 years ago used a lot of available moorstone for their hut circles, in the miles of reaves, for burial in cists, for the many stone rows and stone circles. Later, in the 12th and 13th centuries, many of these antiquities were destroyed and used to build the longhouses and farm buildings, also churches, the hundreds of miles of enclosure walls, and mills and wheelpits for the tin industry. In addition, a great deal of their necessary equipment was made from granite – cheese and cider presses, pig and salt troughs, rollers, gate posts; mortar, mould and float stones; millstones, clapper bridges; mile, guide and boundary stones; artifacts in churches, and of course grave kerb and headstones. Later, when the quarries were opened in the early 19th century, granite was used for many major buildings – London Bridge, Buckingham Palace, New Scotland Yard, Nelson's Column, etc. Locally, of course, Plymouth Breakwater, Tor Royal, Princetown Prison and Church, most of the later buildings in Princetown, and at a much later date, the base for the commemorative obelisk in the Falkland Islands, (which came from Merrivale Quarry).

WALKHAMPTON COMMON

As mentioned previously, Sir Thomas Tyrwhitt was the main instigator for the prison being built, and construction commenced on 20th March 1806 by Isbell, Rowe and Co. The granite for these buildings presumably came from the Herne Hole Quarry, which was within the original 900 acres granted for the prison, although according to the Maristow papers, moorstone was taken from Walkhampton Common. There were numerous disagreements on the exact boundary between the Duchy and Sir Masseh Lopes' Common. One interesting item comes from Burt's Notes in Carrington's *Dartmoor*:

'The commons or wastes of Walkhampton are very extensive being upwards of 10,000 acres, and were the subject of dispute between the Duchy of Cornwall and Sir Masseh Lopes Bart., but, after law proceedings had commenced, the claim of the former was abandoned in March 1810, and subsequently the right of the latter was confirmed by his obtaining a verdict of 500*l*. on a writ of enquiry against Mr Isbell for taking stone therefrom to build Dartmoor prison, without procuring Sir Masseh's leave. In 1820 Sir Masseh granted a lease of the granite thereon to the Plymouth and Dartmoor

Railway Company for a long term of years, which the Company has assigned to Messrs Johnsons and Brice, who are working quarries at King tor, and bringing this handsome and durable material into rapid and extensive circulation.'

The Maristow papers contain many entries regarding encroachment on Walkhampton Common, such as Stephen Kivill in 1789 for 'beginning to hedge and take away part of the Common'; Zachariah Pascho and other contractors for 'making encroachment on North Esworthy Tor' in 1806; Mr Billings for 'cutting and drawing stone from different parts of the Common' and 'person or persons for cutting stone at Ingator and other parts of the Common' in 1820. Some involved Sir Thomas Tyrwhitt:

1822   Sir Thomas Tyrwhitt, Joshua Rowe and others for encroaching on the Common within the last twenty years as ascertained by the boundary line lately marked out.

1824   Sir Thomas Tyrwhitt, Bart. for rising and carrying off sand from the Common.

In addition to the above, are entries concerning boundary stones:

1826   Sir Thomas Tyrwhitt, Rev. J.H. Mason and others for removing the boundary mark at Rundlestone between the land of Sir Manasseh Lopes, Bart. and the Forest.

1831   Mr Minne for removing the Boundary Post on Walkhampton Common and had no right to do so.

1840   The boundary between the Manor and the Forest of Dartmoor as not being properly laid out. The Boundary Posts are improperly placed.

On 13th March 1833, Geo. Giles wrote to Sir Ralph to the effect that he had again written to Mr Johnson who had charged for twelve boundstones which were said to contain 96 feet at 1/-, total £4.16s.0d and a further £3 for drawing and fixing them. 'I recollect there were three of his large horses and several men engaged about the fixing after the stones had been brought to the nearest point by the Railway'. This boundary problem went on for many years.

According to E. Stanbrook in the P&DR Minute Book at PRO, an entry dated 6th July 1824 states that 'Johnson & Brice say they are having difficulty in getting a workforce to quarry the granite'!

METHODS USED IN QUARRYING GRANITE

Contemporary writers of the time have left vivid descriptions of the quarry activities. Bray, for instance, was not at all happy with what he saw on his various 'excursions' - he 'lamented at the spoilations which had been made by the hand of man and the havoc made in these majestic masses of rock'. He did, however, give a good description of the mode of cutting stone after hearing the 'dreadful notes of preparation':

'The mode I had hitherto seen practised for splitting granite was by picking out short longitudinal incisions with a pickaxe, thus - - - -. The method now adopted is to make perforations only, thus ···· And this they do, not by an auger or borer, somewhat like a crowbar, with which (by dropping it with a rotatory motion) they make holes for blasting, that require a larger calibre to contain the charge of powder, but with a lighter and more elegant instrument, being a light rod of iron between four and five feet in length, having a swell or grasp in the centre, thus ——◆——. Indeed, it is not much unlike an ornament occasionally introducted in printing. It makes an acuter sound than that of the common borer, and when two or three are at work with it upon the same block, the sound may be said to be not altogether unmusical. It is astonishing with what precision, after they have lifted it up, that they again dart it into the hole they are deepening.'

The 'older' way of cutting granite was by the wedge system – a line of grooves were chiselled out and wooden wedges, soaked in water, were inserted and which expanded enough to cleave the granite. Later, iron wedges were used, driven home between plates.

R.H. Worth mentioned in his *Dartmoor* that:

'The Rev. E.A. Bray, an observant man, saw the drill in use for the first time within his experience on 17th May 1831, when he visited the quarries at and near Swell Tor. The quarries had then been some years in existence, and no trace can be found among their waste of the use of the older method of working. Doubtless the local men retained their accustomed habit and method for a not inconsiderable time after the introduction of the drill, and there is evidence that the new way of working was not generally established until several years after its introduction. The one safe conclusion is that where it occurs it marks a date not earlier than 1800.'

The author and her husband have walked many miles around the whole complex and have only seen two or three pieces of granite showing the older wedge cuts, one piece having both wedge and feather and tare marks on it, this being on the hillside between Foggintor and North Hessary Tor.

In *Dartmoor Worker* Crossing refers to the Rev. Bray adding:

'The mode of splitting stones now practised is the same as was adopted then, and is called by the workmen 'Feather and Tear'. Holes about 3 inches in depth, or more if necessary, and from 5 inches to 6 inches apart, are drilled in the block required to be split, and into these are inserted wedges, two pieces of thin iron – usually hoop-iron - having previously been placed in each. Between these pieces the wedges are driven, and then successfully struck until the stone is split.'

Dr Peter H. Stanier in his Shire book *Quarries and Quarrying* gives descriptions on quarrying and dressing the stone:

'Widely spaced vertical and horizontal joints enabled large rectangular blocks to be quarried. Deep vertical holes were bored and packed with just enough black powder to displace a block along a horizontal joint without damaging it. Big holes 25 feet (7.6m) deep and 6 inches (150mm) in diameter took many days to bore by hand. Two men struck the heavy boring rod with sledge hammers while two others were needed to give it half a turn between each blow. The introduction of compressed air drills greatly speeded the process.'

'The dressing of granite is an important part of the industry. In the past, a block was first roughly *scappled to* within about two inches (50mm) of its required size with a blocking *hammer.* At first, stones were shipped off in this state, but further dressing soon took place within the quarry or at a yard nearby. *Chisels,* such as the *point tool,* were used for roughing down the stone, while the *chop axe* obtained a finer finish.'

In the 1985 Spring issue of the *Industrial Archaeology Review*, Dr. Stanier writes:

'In early times, only jacks, rollers and crowbars were used to handle granite blocks, but 'crabs' were introduced in the first half of the 19th century and continued in use even after cranes became widespread. In effect, they were portable hand winches which could be anchored securely at a quarry edge and used for dragging stones from parts beyond the reach of a crane. Many cranes, which continued in use well into the 20th century, consisted of a wooden mast, the top of which was supported by six or more strong guys of chain or wire rope, radiating outwards, across the quarry opening to anchor on the edge. The angle of the simple wooden jib was fixed, and a hand winch was attached to either its lower part or the mast. This type of crane had the advantage that it could be swung freely through 360 degrees and could be moved to a new position inside the quarry with relative ease.

All that was required was a strong foundation stone, in which a hole was bored to take the iron-tipped base of the mast'.

There are crane bases at Ingra Tor and Foggintor Quarries.

Derrick cranes were also in existence, many being home-made by quarry blacksmiths and carpenters, and were often in a more permanent position. In the *Report of the British Association For the Advancement of Science,* Part II of 1841, William Johnson wrote the following, 'On the Granite Quarries of Dartmoor and their Railways and Machinery':

'The surface granite of Dartmoor, existing in detached blocks, has been long employed in the neighbourhood for ordinary building purposes, but the quarried granite was first brought into the market by the Haytor Granite Company about the year 1820. The construction of a stone tramway allowed of the granite being shipped at Teignmouth; it now competes with the best Aberdeenshire stone since the lightness of its tint, the fineness of its texture, and the very large blocks in which it can be obtained, render it for some purposes unrivalled, and it has been extensively employed in many public buildings, both in the metropolis and other places, The completion in 1825 of the Plymouth and Dartmoor Railway, of the length of 25 miles and uniform rise of 1 in 94, affords ready transport for the granite of the western face of the moor from Foggintor and other parts adjacent, and the facilities with which these quarries are worked are very great. Strong timber stages with travelling frames and upon the frames powerful traversing crabs, avoiding thereby the labour and delay of lifting by the ordinary means of derricks and cranes, are now in the course of construction. The travelling frames, with the crabs upon them, can be transferred from one line of scaffold to another, so that power may be accumulated to any extent upon one stage, so as to operate on blocks of extraordinary size. The magnitude of the blocks in which the granite can be procured from this quarry, renders it peculiarly fitted for the largest works of the engineer. The beds already accessible lie at great depths below the surface, and yield stone of the greatest compactness, strength and uniformity of colour, and the horizontal disposition of the rock allows of the removal of stone of fair forms and in blocks of the largest size.'

Peter Stanier, writing about 'Granite Quarry Cranes of Cornwall and Devon' for the *Journal of the Trevithick Society* says of the above:

'This apparatus would have been difficult to move as the face advanced or deepened, and it was probably not very successful. It was certainly unique among the granite quarries of the South-West, where few would have been of a suitable size or shape to permit such a construction. There is no evidence at Foggintor today, where several individual crane platforms suggest that single cranes were later found to be more convenient.'

Shown on the Ordnance Survey 1882 25 inch map of the area are three cranes in the larger quarry at Foggintor and one in the smaller one.

To start with, the blocks of granite were roughly shaped and finished off at their destination. The financial advantage gained by dressing granite at, or near, the quarries had been recognised by the 1840s. Some dressing took place at every quarry, but the larger firms had a separate masons yard at a convenient position closer to their markets or at a shipping wharf (Stanier, *I.A. Review*). The Haytor Granite Company (Johnsons) had such a 'works' at Laira, but whether it was used for finishing the dressing is not known.

There were some relevant items in the Maristow papers, the following two being of interest:

31.7.45.   Filmer (Johnsons Agent) called about the Quay at Laira - wants to try a little speculation and import Caen and Portland stone, and would rent the Quay for one year.

25.8.53.   Letter to Filmer from Giles

'The horses drawing the granite from Walkhampton Common to Laira I understand belong to the Haytor Granite Company, whose Agent I believe you are. The wagoners in your employ have lately made a practice of taking off the horses from the wagons on Roborough Down and bringing them round by the Turnpike Road to the end of the lane by Woolwell, they then enter that lane and passed over a private road of Sir Ralph Lopes leading to his woods to the commencement of Fancy Valley, where they again attach the Horses to the loaded wagons. This practice is attended with great damage and inconvenience to Sir Ralph and his tenant at Woolwell and if persevered in must be put a stop to by some more serious proceedings.'

The Johnson Brothers ran the quarries from 1820 to 1865 when the Haytor Granite Co. became Dartmoor Granite Co. (Stanier), and the Bovills presumably took over, at least until 'about 1879' (Crossing) when they sold the railway in the area. The author has been unable to find a date when Pethick Brothers of Plymouth took over the quarries, but it was probably some time in the 1880s.

Quarrying declined in the early years of this century through the importation of Scandinavian granite, and the First World War saw a fall in demand, higher freight charges, lack of ships available, and the introduction of concrete, causing the closing of many quarries. It was a decline which never reversed for buildings, although items such as kerb stones, pillars, gravestones, road metal, etc. were needed, and kept some of the quarries working, albeit in a smaller way.

In 1927 there was a suggestion that Merrivale, Foggintor and Swell Tor quarries should combine under the name of Devonshire Granite Company (Stanier, *I.A. Review*) – it seems strange to include Foggintor which by then had been closed for some twenty years.

There is still a great deal of waste on the various sites, such as Big Tip at Foggintor. According to Peter Stanier 'the winning of granite blocks suitable for engineering and architectural work has always necessitated the discarding of much rock, with as little as 10 per cent of the quarried material being finally used. Large waste tips, with many boulders weighing a ton or more, therefore indicate a quarry worked for such granite'.

The whole complex is well worth a visit, there being still a lot to see, and is again another significant part of Dartmoor's history.

The quarries will now be looked at individually – documentary evidence is very scant, with most of the information covering Swell and Foggintor Quarries.

KING AND INGRA TOR QUARRIES

There is very little mentioned about King Tor apart from the fact that the Plymouth and Dartmoor Railroad had its terminus there until the last section to Princetown was commenced, although Bray does briefly mention it – on leaving Swell Tor, he says:

'King Tor is at some distance, and in going to it, I passed several huts that seemed to be constructed for the use of the labourers; some were little better than mere cavities to shelter them from the heat of the weather. The workmen were principally clustered around and almost hanging (like bees) from what, comparatively speaking, might be called detached rocks, thrown about in a wild and picturesque confusion, but which they will soon reduce to a mere heap of rubbish. The summit of this tor is rather of a bolder cast than the others, with a few recesses which might almost be denominated caves.'

Bray also refers to a quarry where 'they had made a considerable opening at the side, but had not got so deep as in the other. Here instead of an inclined plane, they removed the masses by the mere strength of horses'. This would appear to refer to King Tor also, as the quarry does go in to the base of the tor and it would no doubt be easy enough to have used horses there.

*Clay Works No. 2 Boundary
Stone at Little King Tor
(Dave Brewer)*

*Kerbstones at Ingra Tor
(Brewer Family Photo)*

Looking into Ingra Tor Quarry
(Dave German)

Looking into Ingra Tor Quarry
from above
(Kath Brewer)

View from inside Ingra Tor Quarry

(Elisabeth Stanbrook)

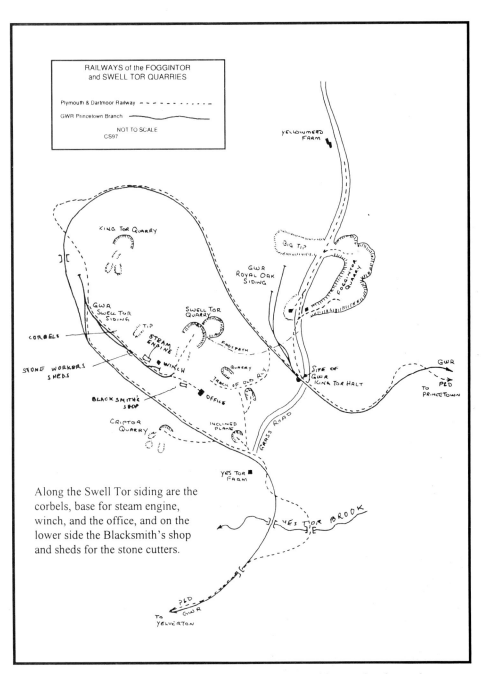

YELLOWMEAD FARM

BIG TIP

KING TOR QUARRY

GWR ROYAL OAK SIDING

FOGGINTOR QUARRY

GWR SWELL TOR SIDING

SWELL TOR QUARRY

CORBELS

TIP

STEAM ENGINE

FOOTPATH

STONE WORKERS SHEDS

WINCH

QUARRY

SITE OF GWR KING TOR HALT

GWR

BLACK SMITH'S SHOP

OFFICE

TRACK OF OLD R.Y.

TO P&D PRINCETOWN

CRIPTOR QUARRY

INCLINED PLANE

GRASS ROAD

Along the Swell Tor siding are the
corbels, base for steam engine,
winch, and the office, and on the
lower side the Blacksmith's shop
and sheds for the stone cutters.

YES TOR FARM

YES TOR BROOK

P&D GWR
TO YELVERTON

Chris Stone's map of the area with one or two additions by the author.

At Little King Tor, the main item of interest is the deviation of the two railway lines, the G.W.R. taking a tighter bend than the P.& D.R. Near the corner of the newtake wall nearby is a boundary stone marked $^{CW}_2$ which appears to be the only remaining boundary stone left referring to a clay sett granted by Sir Ralph Lopes on the 29th September 1835 to George Stone Baron of Plymouth (see *Dartmoor Magazine* 20).

Ingra Tor quarry was very likely worked very soon after Johnson signed the lease. The Maristow papers throw some doubt on this as in both 1820 and 1821 in the Court leet there are presentments for the 'person or persons for cutting stone at Ingator and other parts of the Common belonging to Sir Manaseh Lopes'. However, Bray's (1831) description reads:

'The first (tor) is called (no doubt a corruption of Inga Tor) Innator Tar... On ascending towards it, I could not but lament the spoilation which had been made in it by the hand of man... On a nearer view, the opening occasioned by the deportation of some of these enormous blocks of granite seemed to me like a breach of some Cyclopean fortress, the outer part of the wall that still remained being blackened and worn with weather and with age, whilst the fragments thrown or fallen from it were white and sharp edged. Of these masses scattered below, some were squared, as if for tombs and sepulchres, others reminded me of the teeth of a mammoth... These were such as had been split, and had a serrated appearance, by the holes made in them for the insertion of wedges. This tor appears to have been for some time abandoned by the stone-cutters.'

If the last sentence is correct, Ingra Tor quarry could not have been worked for many years.

There are two crane bases and the remains of a building near the railway which the uncles of the author, and their workmen, used from 1936, when they left Swell Tor, to 1941, when they had a lease from the Maristow Estate to cut kerbstone, granite setts and road metal from the surface stone lying around for Devon County Council. The railway halt was opened for them and their workmen to travel to and from King Tor Halt in March 1936, and also for the transportation of their stone.

SWELL TOR QUARRY

This quarry must also have been working very soon after the lease was signed. To refer to Bray again, he says:

'Passing under some machinery suspended over my head which satisfied me that every recourse had been had to artificial as well as natural powers in this work of destruction, I ascended an inclined plane of great breadth, on which were massy chains running upon rollers, and extending to a considerable distance up the tor. This brought me to another huge mass of machinery equally elevated. This I did not venture to pass, as it was connected with two immense cranes by which the workmen were then employed in poising and depositing on their unwieldy carriages the blocks of granite taken from what might here be called a regular quarry, for they seemed to have laid open the very centre of the tor, whose summit towered perhaps sixty or seventy feet perpendicularly above them. When, by taking a circuit, I got to the top of it and looked down, it was like looking into the bowels of the mountain'

According to Brays 'revised' list of tors, 'the first is called Inga Tor, the second Yeast Tor, the third Swill Tor and the fourth and fifth King Tor and Little King Tor'. If we take the south-east tor on Swell Tor as Yeast Tor (Yestor), this does have an inclined plane, thus the next would be Swell Tor and then along the col to King Tor. This makes sense, and the whole area on the S.E. of the col must have been referred to as Swell Tor at a later date.

LONDON BRIDGE will be looked at in some depth, due to the many conflicting reports as to whether it was Haytor or Foggintor/Swell Tor granite used.

In November 1823 a letter was sent to the engineer of London Bridge protesting that Hay Tor granite was specified and pointing out that similar quality stone from Dartmoor could save £20,000, which of course bore fruit. Hopkins and Johnson went to London for three weeks to tender for the whole construction of London Bridge (but were still there five months later). Referring to Ewans *Haytor Granite Tramway and Stover Canal,* he comments that 'The standard reference book on the subject, *Stones of London,* states that the bridge was built of Princetown Quarry granite, with some from Haytor, but 'the Act of Parliament for the rebuilding' specified three different granites, 'purple' Aberdeen for the eastern side, 'light-grey' Haytor for the western, and to join these together at the arch-stones 'red-brown' Peterhead'. He further states that Haytor granite was 'definitely used on the west face and for the flagstones'. At the grand opening of the Haytor

Tramway on 16th September 1820, George Templer of Stover House was quoted as including the following in his speech: 'In averting to the Plymouth Railway, he expressed his hope that both might prosper, and not endanger, by improper rivalry, the success of either'.

In 1825 George Templer formed a company of the Proprietors of the Devon Haytor Quarries, which later became a joint stock company with capital of £200,000. The company was providing several thousand tons of granite, used in the construction of buildings such as the British Museum, National Gallery, Covent Garden Market, and even some used at Buckingham Palace. In 1829 the house and estate at Stover, the Canal, and also the Haytor Granite Railway was sold to the 11th Duke of Somerset. John Somers Cocks in *D&C N&Q* of 1971 writes:

'What is next related provides the answer to a puzzling question, why the Haytor quarries had closed by 1841 (we know they had from the Ilsington Census Returns for that year) when there was no obvious economic reason for it, and yet had opened again by 1851.

Their Dartmoor rivals were the group of quarries owned by the Johnson brothers at Swell Tor, King Tor and Foggin Tor on Walkhampton Common near Princetown. Their granite was inferior in quality to the Haytor product, and they had failed to get a contract for any part of the building of the new London Bridge in the 1820s. The fact that Haytor granite had been used instead certainly rankled. When the Duke of Somerset let the Haytor quarries in the late 1830s the Johnsons (in the person of John Johnson whom the prospectus describes in 1851 as 'the late Alderman Johnson') secured a seven year lease - and promptly closed them down completely. To add insult to injury they then coolly renamed their own company the Haytor Granite Company, thus not only eliminating all Dartmoor competition but by a nasty piece of misrepresentation passing off their own products as superior to their actual quality. It seems very likely that the renaming accounts for the sometimes quoted belief that some stone for the 1820s building of London Bridge came from the Swell Tor area. It must certainly have caused confusion to the unsuspecting. At the lease's expiry the Duke naturally refused to renew it to the Johnsons......'

However, H.G. Kendall in his *Plymouth and Dartmoor Railway* says that:

'The demand for granite (mentioned in the half-yearly report for December 1827) can be understood when it is realised that Johnsons were the contractors for the Laira Bridge and for surfacing the Breakwater at Plymouth as well as for London Bridge. One of the few engravings showing the railway even vaguely shows the Laira Bridge with the railway and Johnsons Granite works complete with crane in the foreground. It is of interest that a contemporary map shows this as 'Hey Tor Granite Co. Works'.

In the Maristow Papers, the Haytor Granite Co. is not mentioned until the mid-1840s. All rather confusing, particularly as writers invariably state that Walkhampton granite was of a much inferior type to the Haytor granite. However, if a look is taken at the *Mining Journal* of May 1842 referring to Foggintor Quarry, it states:

'It has a beautiful light tint with a fine texture and is available in almost unlimited sizes of block. It is now preferred to Aberdeen granite and was recently used as a base for Chantry's Bronze statue of George IV at Edinburgh and Watt's statue at Glasgow.'

The widening of London Bridge commenced in April 1903, and the following comments appeared in *The Stone Trades Journal* of January 1904:

'All the granite corbels, etc. have been set on both sides of the bridge, and in all there are six hundred and fifty of these large corbels. The length of each is 10 feet by a depth of 3½ feet, and an average width of 1 foot 6 inches, and each has a clear projection or length of leverage 5 feet 6 inches.'

'Nearly the whole of the balusters are in position, and these have been turned by Messrs Pethicks quarries, whilst the granite dies at regular intervals break that which might otherwise perhaps have been somewhat monotonous.'

'Over the corbels, granite slabs are set, which are paved with two layers of Pegrimont Sessell Asphalte half an inch thick, and some 250 feet of York paving has been laid on the west side from the Borough Road.'

'The drainage of the bridge has received careful consideration, formerly no provision whatever was made with the exception of the side scuppers, now, when the surface is cleansed at night the water and refuse will flow into gutters connected by an earthenware pipe 6 inches in diameter, discharging at each end into town drainage.'

'The granite used throughout the whole of the contract has been quarried and worked at the well-known Devonshire quarries of Messrs. Pethick Bros. the contractors. These quarries extend over 2,000 acres and in many places have a face height of 200 feet.'

The fact that this stone has also been selected for the building of the new Vauxhall Bridge is a proof of the favour in which it is held by the authorities, and the quarry installation which comprises a complete outfit of electrical and pneumatic tools and appliances for turning, sawing, dressing and polishing the stone, enables this firm to tender for and secure many of the largest contracts which are offered for competition.

Corbels at Swell Tor Quarry *(Dave Brewer)*

London Bridge at Lake Havasu *(Dave German)*

(Stephen Woods)

Swell Tor Quarry

Wooden Rails at Swell Tor Quarry   *(Elisabeth Stanbrook)*

Ruins of the Blacksmith's Shop, Swell Tor Quarry   *(Elisabeth Stanbrook)*

Ruins of Steam Engine and Compressor Shed, Swell Tor Quarry
(Elisabeth Stanbrook)

'Sailor's Home' Powder House, Swell Tor Quarry (Elisabeth Stanbrook)

The whole of the work is carried out by Messrs. Pethick Bros. the well-known contractors. The engineers are Messrs Murray and Crutwell and Mr Cole is resident engineer. Mr Wm. Muirhead is engineer for Messrs. Pethick Bros.'

There was also a photograph of 'A View of Quarry from which the Granite was Obtained' – the author's relations were very likely in it, but unfortunately the photocopy is too dark to identify individuals.

However, J. Somers Cocks (*Devon and Cornwall Notes & Queries* 1971) writes:

'This time Haytor was the loser and a contract was awarded to Pethick & Co. of Plymouth, the successors in title to the Johnson Brothers at Swell Tor and neighbourhood, who were at work by March 1903 in supplying the stone. Apparently Pethicks had some difficulty in meeting the full demand and so subcontracted part to Duke & Co. at their Merrivale quarry which had opened in 1876. From the Swell Tor quarries the granite was sent down on the Princetown Railway (operated by the G.W.R.) to Pethick's works in Plymouth and then shipped from Cattedown Wharves, but Duke's quarry had greater transportation difficulties. In 1901 teams of powerful horses were still used to take the stone to the L.S.W.R. at Tavistock, but a few years later traction engines towing trailers were employed. The weight of these played havoc with the road down past Moorshop into the town, and the Tavistock Rural Council took the company to Court in about 1907 claiming £4,000 damages for 'extraordinary wear and tear'. They succeeded in obtaining only £1,200.'

Some of the men who worked on the corbels at Swell Tor were the Ruby Brothers (the author's grandfather and uncles), Chippy Hext, Eli Eva, Harry and Sam White, Mousey Rook, Dave Rook, Charlie and Sam Gill, also Perkins, Williams, Easterbrook and Cooper (Dr T. Greeves).

There are two versions regarding the corbels remaining by the railway siding at Swell Tor – the author was told by the late blacksmith at Swell Tor that they were condemned due to iron marks in them; the other version is that they were cut too short. It did not stop some of them being loaded on to lorries by a mobile crane when London Bridge was dismantled and transported to America.

There was an interesting report in the *Western Morning News* of 6th December 1995, stating that the Bridge was sold to oil tycoon Robert McCulloch, (on 18th April 1968) for three million pounds, but he thought he was getting Tower Bridge. Due to the cost of transporting it, quarry workers at Merrivale Quarry had to cut the stones, leaving the facing blocks, which were then sent to Lake Havasu City in Arizona in 1971, where a false river bed had been excavated. A concrete replica was built, narrowing the original by 15 feet, and cut into three sections so it could expand in the Arizonian heat. When one of the workmen who had been involved on this project returned to Merrivale Quarry after an absence of just over twenty years, he found most of the remains of the old bridge were still at the Quarry, covered by grass and undergrowth. More layers were stacked at the side of the Quarry and some had even been built into the quarry walls.

Finally, on the saga of London Bridge, an account of the 'Bridge Feast' appeared in the *Western Morning News* of 28th October 1996:

'ARIZONA; Bagpipe players, a medieval show and a two and-a-half ton cake helped celebrate the rededication of London Bridge in Arizona.

Twenty-five years ago British dignitaries feasted on crab and shrimp, and up to 100,000 revellers gathered to dedicate the bridge. After more than a century of spanning the Thames in London, the granite bridge was dismantled block by block, shipped across the ocean and reassembled in the Arizona desert. Lake Havasu City has been holding a week-long extravaganza to commemorate the 1971 dedication of the bridge.'

The author's grandfather was killed in an accident at the quarry on 29th March 1919. He was in charge of the turning over of a lump of granite, standing at the head of the quarry where the chain was attached to a steel ring. The cable from a crane in the bottom of the quarry, and the 'dog' were in position, when the 'dog' slipped, entangling the chain around him, causing him to be thrown to the bottom of the quarry. He received severe head injuries and died almost immediately.

The 'dog' is the large 'hook' which helps to turn the granite, shaped thus

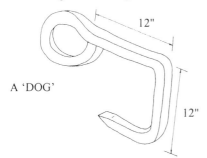

A 'DOG'

12"

12"

the steel in the 'dog' is about 4" square.

Other accidents happened, such as when powder ignited whilst being 'tamped' down killing one workman and causing another to lose an eye. The dusty work did not do the workmen's health any good, and led to many chest complaints.

The south-west siding junction was controlled by a Ground Frame, whose conspicuous yellow box could be seen from quite a distance. The remains of the buildings alongside the sidings, past the corbels, are a weighbridge where in later years granite chippings were weighed before being transported for use as railway line ballast, and in the 1930s ballast was sent for sea defences at Dawlish Warren. There were stone cutters sheds, a mechanical crusher housed in a galvanised shed, a concrete base where a building housed the large Steam Compressors from the late 1920s or early 1930s – they provided air under pressure built up in a huge drum to work various pneumatic drills; the blacksmith's shop which was on the lower side of the rails with the Foreman's office just above. There was a small building called the 'Sailors Home' at the top of the quarry where the explosives were kept (Mead).

Dr Stanier mentioned that the prospectus of the Devonshire Granite Co. Ltd. was formed by Duke of Merrivale Quarry in 1927, and incorporated that quarry and Swell Tor. C. Sellick was a director of this company. I have recently heard from John Tonkin regarding the installation of two Fieldings 80hp machines – from his conversations with his late father he thinks the date would probably be 1934 but could possibly have been a year or two earlier. Claude Sellick, who went to the St Austell area as a clayworks manager before the Great War, was the youngest son of Christopher Sellick, originally a clay captain for Martin Brothers at Lee Moor but later re-opening Wotter Waste Clayworks on his own account. Claude had interests in two Dartmoor quarries, Merrivale and Swell Tor, and it was decided to mechanise them. John's late father stayed at the Dartmoor Inn, Merrivale, whilst supervising the foundations, counter shafting and other work required for the two machines which were to drive air compressors, and Mr Tonkin also converted the steam derricks in the quarries to work on compressed air, but Fielding employees saw to the actual installation of their engines.

Quarrying at Swell Tor continued on a large scale, and about ninety men were employed until the First World War. With the increasing use of concrete for the building industry, quarrying declined. The quarry has been reported as closing in the twenties but re-opening in 1937 for a short period. Albert Mead told me that Swell Tor was still working when my uncles opened Ingra Tor, and he thought it finally closed in 1938.

THE SIDINGS

Before Foggintor Quarry is dealt with, let us take a look at the Sidings and layout of the railway. The map on page 47 shows what can be seen on the ground at present – of course, it must be borne in mind that in the 180 years or so since the quarries and railroad opened, there must have been a number of alterations, although many of the Plymouth and Dartmoor setts are still in situ.

Ingra Tor is shown as having two short sidings on one map, but this has not been checked, although from memory they would appear to be roughly where the later building used by my uncles was situated.

At the south side of Swell Tor is an inclined plane – even in Bray's day (1830s) there was an inclined plane in this vicinity – and next, on the opposite side of the railway track, is a siding to a small quarry (Criptor Quarry), with setts in situ. On the northeast side of the railway, just below King Tor, is the 'main' siding which runs south-east past the corbels and ruined buildings low down on Swell Tor, with one or two possible branches off it. The next sidings are on the north-east side of Swell Tor where three 'tracks' are marked on O.S. maps. One is marked as 'Footpath' and goes to the main quarry. The middle one is marked as 'Track of Old Railway' on a map which still shows the G.W.R. Railway, but marks Walkhampton Foggintor School as (Disused) and the Headmasters' House as 'Fourwinds', so it must be after 1938. The third one (from King Tor Halt to the railway track near Yestor Farm) is marked 'Grass Road'. Another map (with the date 1982 written on it) shows the school as a ruin, the footpath is no longer marked, and 'The Track of Old Railway' and the G.W.R. track all as 'Dismantled Railway'. The 'Track of the Old Railway' section still has a double row of setts in situ. As a matter of interest, here the setts seem to be in sections of 15-16 feet in length with the stones thus: (Ambrose)

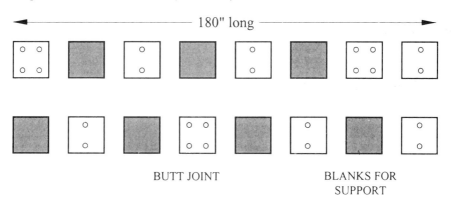

BUTT JOINT   BLANKS FOR SUPPORT

The setts with no holes are presumably for support, and they are either round or square in shape. No setts have been found on the 'footpath' which is to be expected if that is all it ever was - an easy way to get to the quarry face for the workmen from Hill Cottages.

On the opposite side of the railway is a possible siding along to the main Foggintor Quarry, where the section into the quarry is now very wet. Crossing

The Archway at Foggintor   *(Chris Stone)*

The Archway at Ynys y Pandy Slate Mill,
Gorseddau Quarry, Wales   *(Chris Stone)*
Both have flat areas on top of the well built walls as far back as the arches.

*The ruined building above the archway, showing the flat area, with the entrance
to the smaller Foggintor Quarry* *(Chris Stone)*

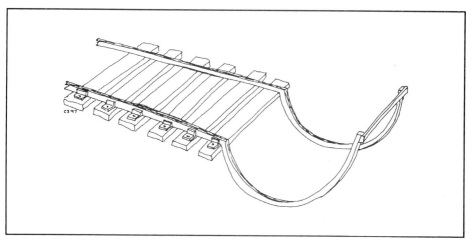

Diagram of rail used for tipping granite off the trucks *(Chris Stone)*

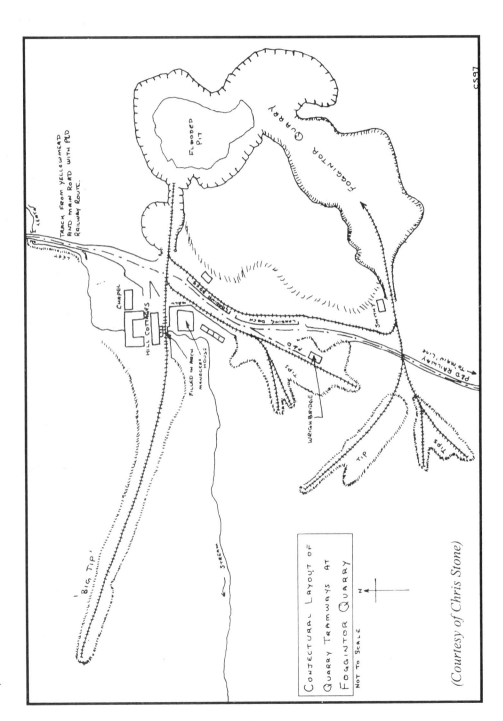

CS97

TRACK FROM YELLOWMEAD AND MAIN ROAD WITH PLD RAILWAY ROUTE.

FLOODED PIT

FOGGINTOR QUARRY

CHAPEL

HILL COTTAGES

FILLED IN PATH

MANAGERS HOUSE

LOADING BACK

FOGGIN DEPOT

PLD

TIP RD

WEIGHBRIDGE

SMITHY

PLD RAILWAY 'TO MAIN LINE

TIP

TIPS

'BIG TIP'

STREAM

CONJECTURAL LAYOUT OF QUARRY TRAMWAYS AT FOGGINTOR QUARRY

NOT TO SCALE

N

(Courtesy of Chris Stone)

— 62 —

The northern side of Big Tip with the ruins of Eva's farm to the right, and King Tor in the middle distance (Chris Stone)

The southern side of Big Tip with Merrivale Quarry to the left, and Staple and Roos Tors in the distance (Chris Stone)

(Stephen Woods)

Foggintor Quarry

— 64 —

Foggintor Quarry showing the depth to which the granite had been removed

(Stephen Woods)

Boggy entrance where the original P & D.R. track with setts would have entered
(Chris Stone)

One of the Crane Bases at Foggintor Quarry   *(Elisabeth Stanbrook)*

Another Crane Base at Foggintor Quarry
(Elisabeth Stanbrook)

P. & D.R. setts in track, taken near
Yellowmead Farm looking towards Foggintor
(Elisabeth Stanbrook)

refers to Foggintor Quarry and another, Higher Quarry, 'near some cottages', which are presumably (Red) Cottages, as he never seemed to mention Hill Cottages anywhere, so this could possibly be Hollow Tor. The main railroad started near the later King Tor Halt and virtually followed the lane to the Mission Hall, which is confirmed by someone who was an apprentice at Swell Tor during the 1926 General Strike. The apprentices had to be kept occupied and first they cleared the leat from its source along to Hill Cottages, and when this was done, they had to repair the track. Starting at the Mission Hall end of the track they removed the granite sleepers and broke them up for the foundations for the road. They only got roughly as far as Yellowmead Farm when the Strike was called off and they had to return to work again at Swell Tor.

There is also the question of the use of Royal Oak as a name. The first mention is as Royal Oak Siding at 8m 75 chs on the Siding Layout of the late 1890s (see Kingdom's *The Princetown Branch*). After that date, Foggintor Quarry, the Chapel and even the 'weighbridge bungalows' were known as Royal Oak, Crossing and Rowe both using the name. It is obvious this is a G.W.R. name and nothing to do with the earlier Plymouth and Dartmoor Railway, as Royal Oak has not appeared in any of the older documents/books referred to. Royal Oak Siding consisted of a cutting from near King Tor Halt, swinging due north into two sections with raised embankments, ending well up towards Big Tip but with a short section off to the east, towards other spoil tips. The field at the end below Big Tip at one time belonged to Billie Rich, who was general foreman at Swell Tor; he had a shed as a stable and kept a couple of ponies there.

FOGGINTOR QUARRY

Foggintor was first mentioned in the 1408 Assize Rolls as Vokketorre (*Place Names of Devon* 1931); other spellings include Vokaton, Fogator, Foggaton,etc.

My family lived in the house above the built-up archway at Hill Cottages, and I have always been fascinated by it and hoped to one day discover what it was originally. I have not been able to find any documents to enlighten me, but since January 1996 I have received various letters from Chris Stone, who is mainly interested in Welsh mines and quarries, but knowing of my interest in Foggintor, put forward the most sensible explanation I have heard on its existence. The suggestion was that at an early period in the quarry's life it had been used for a water-wheel, and he enclosed photocopies showing a similar structure at Ynys y Pandy Slate Mill, Gorseddau Quarry. It is disappointing to state that further research has still proved fruitless. Unfortunately, I have also been unable to find a date for the cutting of the leat, although in the Maristow papers, when the Mount Pleasant (Red) cottages were proposed in 1847, there was a clause that the water 'be applied to household purposes only, and not to the working of any kind of machinery and the quantity so limited should be the minimum of the required supply, Sir Ralph wishing to retain the command of water as much as possible for other purposes should it be required'. This could imply that the leat had been used for machinery before, but probably not then, as there were only two 'unofficial' houses at Foggintor as will be seen in Part 3. It is also doubtful that money would have been spent on cutting a leat other than for industrial use.

Chris Stone's first impression on seeing the archway was that it had once been a mill, being similarly situated to Gorseddau where 'This mill was built partly on a waste tip and partly on a hillside, and water was conducted through the building to operate a breast shot waterwheel which in turn operated line shafting for the saws, etc. The tail race from the wheel consisted of two stone retaining walls with a straddling arch to support the mill wall'. The two retaining walls of the archway at Foggintor had large dressed stone blocks laid in courses and neatly done, and must by logic have been there first. The building above was small undressed stone rubble held together with cement and the archway constructed in the same materials. Largish stone blocks with smaller stones towards the top were used, not in courses but haphazardly for the infill and were laid to suit the opening without any of the corner stones being keyed into the retaining walls.

From photographs Chris took at Gorseddau, the main mill wall and arch is some 8-9 feet behind the end of the pit walls which is very similar to Foggintor, and the waterwheel would be in behind the tailrace portal. Chris paid another visit to Foggintor in October 1996, and found that the retaining wall seemed to return on itself, but could not see enough to say how far it went. A waterwheel that utilised a small flow but largish volume (like a slow flowing river) would be of broad rather than narrow construction. The wheelpit at Foggintor may be about ten feet wide which equates quite nicely with other High Dartmoor waterwheels, such as the one at Golden Dagger Mine. It would be the weight of water on the buckets that caused the wheel to turn, not the force with which the water hit the wheel – it just needed sufficient water to reach the wheel. Chris also sent his ideas (totally conjectural he says) on the layout of the quarry tramways, which would of course have been prior to the houses being built, but which looks very probable.

A waterwheel could have been used for power for bellows at a Smith or Foundry, which may well have been sited within the machine shop, but the pit appears to be too small for this on its own, or alternatively, it could have been used for stone cutting or pumping machinery, or even for a flat rod system to pump out the larger quarry. Pumps could have been worked by flat rods and bell cranks or by wire ropes from a remote waterwheel. The small entranceway between the two quarries could have been the passageway for rods or ropes from a waterwheel to a pump, and could also have been used for the removal of waste.

Presumably by 1841 the quarry had been so busy that Big Tip had been virtually built to the size one sees today, as on 10th September 1841 Geo Giles visited the quarry and wrote the following:

'A great number of men were at work… about 300… and much expensive and powerful and well contrived machinery erected… five machines acting on the principles of Cranes and traversing on Rails placed on a frame work… also a long building supported on tall granite posts with the sides and Roof formed of Boards well coated with Tar; wherein I found about twenty Smiths busily at work – a comfortable stalled Stable is attached at one end of this Building. Not far from this is another similarly constructed… used as a workshop for Carpenters and Turners… a wing attached to this Building serves as an Office and Store House for Tools and Materials… In another part I found a number of men engaged in facing up with a stone wall of considerable thickness and strength a heap of Rubbish brought out of the Quarry, on the summit of which I was told an extensive Shed was to be erected under the Roof and shelter of which the Stone Masons may work in all weathers.'

This latter could very well be the building above the archway which was altered for housing later.

There have been a number of rumours regarding the use of the archway, such as to store the explosives, which seems ludicrous; it had a railway through; and ponies pulled trucks through it. In fact, Albert Mead told me his grandfather, Samuel Hext, who worked at Hill Quarries, said that the granite wagons were stored in there until the quarry closed and the opening blocked up.

I again quote from Chris Stone's correspondence regarding the gauge of the quarry wagons:

'The P.& D. was, I think, 4 feet 6 inches and the GWR 4 feet 8½ inches which explains the width of the blocks on the Yellowmead track. However, it would have been likely that the tramways within the quarry were about 2 feet or thereabouts, that gauge being easier to re-lay as work advanced and smaller wagons were easier to manhandle. The line used to take spoil to the end of Big Tip could not have been much wider as the usual way of tipping rubbish was to have end tipping wagons and a section of rails shaped thus at the extreme end of the line. (see page 61)

As the wagon's leading wheels dropped into the depressions stopping it 'dead', the workmen simultaneously pushed upwards on the trailing end and shot the rubbish out of the wagon. A wagon larger than about 2 feet gauge (holding around 2 tons of spoil) would have been too heavy to handle by one man. Obviously a horse could pull more, or two men could handle a heavier load.'

Bray has some further observations on this area:

'On ascending the hill from Merrivale Bridge, I observed some kind of vehicle taking a most unusual direction from the road, apparently among the Druidical circles or rather the cursus. I certainly did not take it for an ancient British chariot, not only because it moved but slow, but also because it had a head, or awning. I almost fancied it a cargo of antiquaries, or at least a party of pleasure come to explore the antiquities of the spot, but, on approaching nearer, I found it was a cart laden with hay. On returning to the railroad, I hesitated whether I would not pursue a branch of it that led to a quarry in the side of a hill under Hessary Tor. I was somewhat desirous to discover whether it was worked open or excavated, particularly as it coincided with my theory that there was no necessity to demolish the tors themselves, but the fog was again coming on, and I thought it more prudent to curtail my excursion. Near this branch road is a long shed, in which, from the sounds that came from it, I had reason to believe that many were employed in hewing into form the blocks that had been brought from this quarry. And indeed I could not but conclude that it afforded harder and larger masses than those I had visited on the summits of the tors, as I saw immense columns lying near, which I understood from one of the workmen, were to be employed in the construction of some market in London.'

No doubt it can be assumed the 'cart of hay' would be used to feed the horses at the quarries, but where exactly did Bray go? The assumption that after 'climbing the hill from the bridge' he took the Tavistock/Ashburton track towards the haycart in the cursus, but crossed the Longash Brook to get to the railroad. On walking along it towards Princetown he came to a 'branch road' which would imply the 'long shed' was near the bottom of the track to Foggintor, and could possibly be the one mentioned by Geo. Giles in 1841.

Bray's diaries were from May 1831 when the quarries appeared to have been very busy. However, in October 1832, Geo. Giles wrote:

'Fox seems unable to account for the Slackings of the Granite Trade on the Rail Road in any other way than that it is the case with Business in

General. Great stagnation he says prevails in every department. The Limestone Quarries at Plymouth have been for several weeks shortening their hands very considerably.'

In 1846 Rachel Evans wrote *Home Scenes of Tavistock and its Vicinity*, and on returning from Princetown to Tavistock, she gave her impression of the area as follows:

'A carriage road conducts the curious to the granite quarries by some of the most delightful views which can be afforded by the moorland district. Successive Tors vie with each other in grandeur, until they are replaced by the blue Cornish Hills, with the promontory of Mount Edgcumbe and the silvery line of the ocean in the distance. The quarries to which we now direct our attention are hidden from view, until the spectator is close upon them. At one moment he looks over the dreary moor without observing a human being, in another an immense excavation presents itself studded with workmen, as busily employed as bees in the hive; some are boring holes in the flinty rock, others are filling the cavities with powder, some are chipping the rude blocks into shape; others are lifting their ponderous weight by cranes and levers; horses, carts and railroad waggons are in constant employment to convey away the heavy masses of stone (some 20 feet in length) which have been made available in the principal works of the metropolis; the Post Office, London Bridge, and the Houses of Parliament have been constructed by this strong material. Three hundred men were formerly in constant work on the spot; their work is very laborious, as the granite is very coarse grained, and brittle. The blacksmiths are always busily employed in sharpening tools blunted by the stone.

A difficult road across the moor, suited only to travellers on horseback, conducts a route of two miles to Merrivale Bridge.'

Quarrying must have picked up again by then, as other constructions also used the granite from this complex, including Nelson's Column.

Sett Makers Bankers are very common around the Staple Tors area. A 'Sett Makers Banker' comprises two upright pieces of granite with another piece across the top, and the workmen probably knelt at or possibly stooped over the 'table' to work. Larger pieces of granite were broken and cut to a size of 18 inches x 9 inches and 5 inches thick, which the Sett Makers then chipped away at to make the required smaller sized blocks, which were used as setts in roads, kerbstones, etc, in places such as Tavistock and Plymouth. When looking at Foggintor Quarry, my husband and I only found one Banker. However, in December 1996, our friend Ted Fitch wrote to say he and his wife found over a dozen at Foggintor and about half that number (on a single short visit) at Swell Tor. No doubt there are more to be found, although probably some are under the various spoil tips. Ted went on to say that there seem to be three categories of Bankers: 1) where they are grouped together with well built (originally) shelter walls, as on Mid Staple Tor; 2) where they are situated in the open, but in seemingly neighbourly groups, as along the Grimstone & Sortridge Leat above Merrivale; 3) where they are isolated from each other, as at Foggintor and Swell Tor.

In the Staple Tors area various forms of Bankers are to be found back to back, at right angles to each other, in groups of three or four. Some appear to be so close together that it would probably be impossible for more than one man to work at a time.

Foggintor Quarry has been referred to as Hill Quarry, the same as the nearby cottages, but no trace was found of the source of this name. However, Basil Thomson in his *The Story of Dartmoor Prison* (1907) mentions that on November 1st 1850, the 4th Regiment under Ensign Hall marched into Princetown, and the following day was despatched to Hill Quarry to meet 59 convicts from Millbank, this according to Rhodes (*Dartmoor Prison 1806-1932*), being the month when the first drafts of convicts arrived.

There were also quarries further along the track towards the main road and smaller outcrops, which have been worked, also no doubt a great deal of moorstone was removed which would account for the Plymouth & Dartmoor Railroad putting setts right along this track. In the Maristow papers under Water and Mine Rents, the following appeared:

Oswald Easterbrook ⎫
James Claude Rooke ⎬ Granite Works, Rundlestone
William Stephens ⎭
29th September 1919. 20 years mm. Rent £5 in advance. Due.

Dave German tells me that in 1936 Hill 60 (Hollow Tor) Quarry was opened by Billy Easterbrook, Claude Rook and Alf Brown, labourer. Was the quarry opened in 1919 at Hollow Tor, and if so, where did Easterbook and Rook go until Hollow Tor was 're-opened' in 1936? I do not know how long Hollow Tor remained open after 1936.

There is also another quarry on the west side of the track, behind the Red Cottages ruins, on which a lease was held by my uncles from 1941 when they left Ingra Tor. This quarry, West Mead, continued to be worked, later by my cousins, until its final closure in 1966. The quarry had its own blacksmith's shop, the bellows of which Simon Ford, a Dartmoor Park Ranger at the time, on one of the

(Stephen Woods)

Foggintor Quarry showing lines where huge blocks of granite have been removed

Another view of Foggintor Quarry   *(Chris Stone)*

The platform from which granite was loaded on to the trucks   *(Chris Stone)*

Looking at the ruins of Royal Oak Bungalows. This was formerly the Weighbridge, and setts can still be seen veering towards the ruin   *(Chris Stone)*

Showing the beginning of more granite tips and the ruin of Royal Oak Bungalows
(Chris Stone)

A single sett maker's banker, Foggintor Quarry *(Dave Brewer)*

A double sett maker's banker, Foggintor Quarry *(Elisabeth Stanbrook)*

West Mead Quarry   *(Dave German)*

Ruins of crane/jib platform, West Mead Quarry   *(Dave German)*

Site of Blacksmith's Shop, West Mead Quarry, with one of the last lessees
(Dave German)

Ruined building at Criptor Quarry   *(Elisabeth Stanbrook)*

Criptor Quarry (Elisabeth Stanbrook)

Rail Road showing sett still in situ,
Criptor Quarry
(Elisabeth Stanbrook)

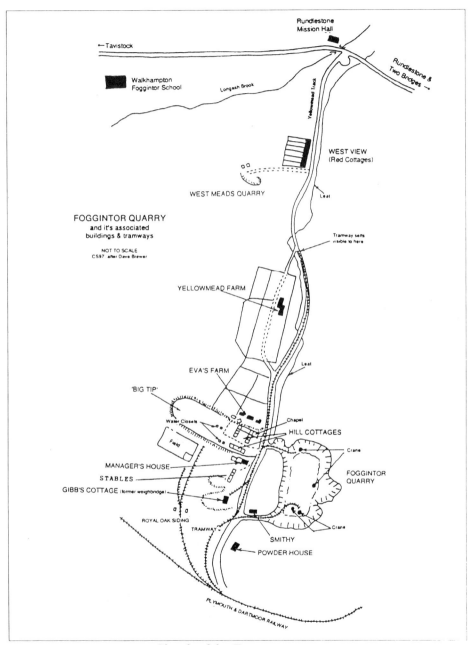

Sketch of the Foggintor area.
Drawn by Chris Stone, based on an earlier sketch by Dave Brewer

DNP's 'clean-up' efforts, took to Tavistock Museum (Ambrose). To the south of Hill Cottages, further along the track were a few partly worked artifacts which were produced by my cousins when 'learning their trade'.

We will come to the end of this section with a few quotes from various Maristow papers:

On the 19th February 1856, Geo Giles wrote to Filmer:

'I have received information that diverse persons around Princetown have of late been taking quantities of stones for building purposes from Sir Ralph Lopes Commons on the Hill between Haytor Granite Company and Princetown.

The authorities at the Prison it is stated are also taking considerable quantities of paving stones from the neighbourhood of Mis Tor, decidedly within Sir Ralph Lopes boundary.

Now I request you will inform me whether these stones so taken by the parties referred to have been so taken in consequence of an arrangement by them with the Haytor Granite Company or otherwise.'

The following come from the Estate Agents Diary:

1899	June 6	Inspected Quarry at Princetown.
1900	Sept 11	Pethicks Quarry, etc.
1901	Apr 17	Princetown Granite Quarry. Examined working of Quarry and stone produced.
1902	Apr 29	Foggintor Quarry. Mr Pethick examined these quarries with the manager. Very great developments have been made during the last two years and the quarries are now looking very well. A large amount of stone is being raised for Vauxhall Bridge and London Bridge, and also for the Pembroke Docks. They are speaking of putting on another 50 men.
1903	Mar 25	Pethicks Quarry. Looked around
	June 23	Quarry. Mr Pethick had a good look around.
	July 27	Princetown Quarry. It is very evident that Messrs Pethick intend to take out as much stone as possible before the end of their Lease at Michaelmas 1906. They are enlarging the face of the quarry and have a very large staff employed.
1904	Apr 4	Princetown Quarries. No work being done and very little dressed stone on the ground. A good deal of stone is raised in the quarry.

1905	Oct	24	Trade is said to be very slack in the meantime and only a small staff is being worked.
1906	June	22	Granite Quarries. There have been several contracts secured lately and all the old hands are again not working all the machinery but to be started again on Monday.
	July	27	With Mr Lopes at Pethicks Quarry and Walkhampton Common.

This is the last entry found, and Foggintor Quarry closed down at Michaelmas 1906. This is when large timbers were put in under the houses to secure them and the archway blocked up – which seems a bit late when the building above was erected just after 1841 and made into dwellings before 1851!

The sketch of the area was drawn by my husband, Dave, many years ago, kindly re-drawn for me by Chris Stone, and virtually speaks for itself. The powder house was stone built with a heavy steel door to it, with granite slabs inside for stowing the explosives on. Unfortunately, I have not found any ruins which look substantial enough for this, but anything could have happened to the stone used since the quarry closed ninety years ago.

As a child, I recall being told never to go into the big quarry – the small one was all right – so my first visit to it, which must have been in the sixties, was quite an experience and eye-opener!

**

Before we leave the Quarries, there is another small one which is situated to the west of Swell Tor, on the opposite side of the railway, which we will call Criptor Quarry, for want of a better name. No reference was found to this quarry at all, but it must have been in use comparatively early, as there are tramway setts still in situ.

**

On page 40, William Crossing mentions 'Feather and Tear' whereas the spelling normally used is 'Tare'. On checking 'Tare' in Chambers Dictionary, the meanings are given as 'any one of several species of vetch', or 'the weight of the vessel or package in which goods are contained', or 'obsolete pa. p. of tear'. Looking at 'Tear' it gives 'to draw asunder or separate with violence, to make a violent rent in', and, for the pa.p. the explanation is 'torn, something torn, a rent', which is not really the best description for the quarry workers method for 'breaking' large pieces of granite!

PART 3: THE COTTAGES

The 1795 Survey of Walkhampton Manor shows no holdings at Rundlestone or Foggintor, and none at Foggintor on the 1840 Tithe Map.

On looking through various Maristow papers, the first cottage appears to have been built between 1808-10 when we find a John Carter paying rent of £5 for 'a newbuilt house and 20 acres of ground between Rundlestone and Little Mis Tor'. This continues in the records, but by the new ledger in 1821 we find he owes £13.10.0 from the last ledger. However, by 1824 the house is in ruins and that part of Walkhampton Common is 'enclosed in Prison Lands'. In 1836 he is being presented for rebuilding a 'Cot House' on the Common, but in 1837 he is being presented for 'an encroachment' by building a house, and paid 5/- as an acknowledgment. In June 1841, Geo. Giles, Agent for the Lopes family, wrote a letter to R. Burnard, as follows:

'John Carter has no interest in the Hut and Land he occupies at Walkhampton... but he holds it merely on sufferance. The fact is, in the year 1806 the late Sir Masseh Lopes granted a lease of a piece of Common Land to Carter for a term, on condition of his erecting and afterwards keeping in repair certain Buildings and Fences and paying a reserved rent. The Lease contained a proviso that if the premises became dilapidated to the value of 20/- and were not repaired within three months next after notice to that effect, the Lord should have a right to re-enter. In 1821 the premises became greatly dilapidated and a large arrear of Rent was due... the whole of the Buildings fell into a mass of ruins, the Land reverted to and became part of the Common. Carter disappeared and was not seen for many years afterwards, but about three or four years since the Jury of the Court Leet made a presentment that John Carter had tresspassed on the Common by erecting a hut and inclosing a piece of ground. Carter was called upon to answer... petitioned to be suffered to remain in his hut, which Sir Ralph Lopes, commiserating his subject state, permitted him to do, on his paying Five Shillings a year as an acknowledgment during Sir Ralph Lopes pleasure.'

The Tavistock to Moretonhampstead road was turnpiked by two Acts of 1772, although the road probably was not completed for a number of years. Crossing in 'One Hundred Years on Dartmoor' says:

'The making of a portion of the road from Tavistock to Moretonhampstead was contracted for by an aged Moorman named Carter, who lived in a rude hut near Rundle Stone and who, with his sons, carried out the work.'

In all probability this refers to John Carter. The Rundlestone was a 7 foot menhir which stood roughly opposite to the obtuse angle boundary stone with Lidford and Walkhampton on it, on the north side of the road. This was placed there erroneously by the Turnpike Trust, as these Trusts had to erect 'parish' stones wherever their roadway crossed parish bounds. This boundary stone could have added to the confusion on the line of the boundary from North Hessary Tor to Great Mis Tor over the years, as could the one between the land of Sir Masseh Lopes and the Forest in 1826 when Sir Thomas Tyrwhitt, Rev. J.H. Mason and others were presented for removing a boundary mark in the Rundlestone area (see page 38).

There were disputes between the Duchy and Walkhampton on this boundary for about 150 years, with it formerly following the wall, and it was not until 1867 that a Deed of Agreement was drawn up between the Duchy and Lopes to define the boundary and mark north Hessary Tor and Great Mis Tor with iron 'crosses' (or 'cobra heads', which is a better description!), inscribed WB and FB (Walkhampton and Forest Bounds), this boundary being the present line. On the 1240 Perambulation this section was 'a straight line' between these two tors.

An interesting aspect here is that Carter rented land on Walkhampton Common, but it is also mentioned as being 'enclosed on Prison Land'. The Prison land was only about 900 acres originally, and the boundary went from North Hessary Tor to Little Tor and then crossed the Princetown Road. About 1867 their land was enlarged by approximately 1000 acres and the prison boundary then followed the wall from North Hessary, past the obtuse angle boundary stone, then up to the Mis Tor Farm where it deviated around some of their land before re-joining the Forest/Walkhampton boundary as far as New Forest Corner. With the boundary making a curve instead of continuing as a straight line, the assumption that Carter's cottage was where this deviation occurred is most probably correct. A John Eva had been presented in 1841, 1843 and 1848 for building a cottage without permission either 'near Carters' or 'near Rundlestone', the 1848 item being for 'enclosing land on Walkhampton Common near Rundlestone'. The only family at Rundlestone on the 1851 census was that of Richard Eva, his wife 'Honner', sons John (3) and Eli (2) and brothers Samuel and Thomas. They were probably at Wheal Lucky, where they were on later Census Returns, but there was no mention of John Eva. By 1861 eleven families were there, one being John Eva farming 40 acres, with his family which included an 18 year old daughter Selena, at Mount Pleasant. The Burial Registers of Walkhampton Parish contain an entry dated 8th October 1871 when John Eva died at Mis-Tor Farm, and on 8th May 1879 when Selena Vinnicombe (aged 37) died at Rundlestone, both bearing the comment 'Debateable Ground between the Parishes of Lydford and

Walkhampton'. (M. Brown). Mis Tor Farm is where the prison boundary deviated and so could be classed as 'debateable' and possibly 'enclosed in prison land'. The last reference to John Carter is his burial at Princetown in 1843, and in 1841 Eva was building 'near Carters' so it seems conclusive that this is the area in which they both built homes.

In 1813 we have Henry Eva paying £1 'for an encroachment on the Common near Rundle Stone', and over a number of years, to at least 1848, there are presentments for Henry erecting a house either 'near Carters', 'near Stone Tor', 'near Rundlestone', or just 'on Walkhampton Common' with mention of two acres of land from 1835, and in 1848 for 'enclosing land on Walkhampton Common near Rundlestone'. In the Duchy Records there is a map, dated 1852, showing 'Double Thatch Cottage' (Rendell), occupied by William Eva, and stated as being in the 'Parish of Lidford'. The buildings are slightly downhill from Rundlestone Tor (it is possible that this tor was called Rock Tor, Stone Tor being the nearby Hollow Tor) but by the wall of the 'old' boundary, and consequently between the two disputed boundaries. In actual fact, we find the Duchy leasing the sliver of land from North Hessary Tor to Rundlestone between these two boundaries in 1852, prior to the Deed of Agreement of 1867.

In 1840, the Haytor Granite Company were presented for 'Building a House near Foggaton, having no right to do so' and William Williams was also presented for 'Building a House and enclosing Land near Foggaton Quarry'.

The Williams family (William and Mary) were at Yes Tor in 1838, but he was building a house at Foggintor in 1840. In a letter to Sir Ralph, dated 10th September 1841, Geo Giles wrote:

'...there is a most substantially built Cottage with stone walls and Verandah thatched roof containing six comfortably fitted rooms wherein Mr Johnson at times spends his week. An addition to the cottage is in progress... for a kitchen and other offices.

At a short distance I saw another Cottage on a smaller scale which I understand had been erected by one of the workmen of the name of William Williams for his own residence, and a large piece of ground enclosed by a Hedge (the extent approaching to nearly an acre) and cropped with Potatoes which looked in a thriving and healthy condition.'

(We will concentrate on the Williamses now and refer to the Johnson building later). William and Mary had a daughter named Rosina, and on the 1881 Census Return, a Henry Eva and his wife Rosina are shown as living at Foggintor. By the 1891 Census, a Mary Williams, mother-in-law, was also a member of the household. This ties in nicely with 'Eva's Farm' just to the north of Hill Cottages, which according to the details Elisabeth Stanbrook sent from the Public Record Office document, was as follows:

Part Foggintor. Farm. l3a,lr,6p (13 acres, 1 rood, 6 perch)

Gross value: land £9.l0s; buildings £2.l0s.

Owner: Sir Henry Lopes, Bart.

Interest of Owner: Freehold.

Occupier's Tenancy Term: Yearly

Occupier: H. Eva

"12.934 Moorland Pasture - 353 House Bldgs & Yard. Old stone build (sic) house with wood & felt roof, bungalow.

Ground Floor - 3 rooms & lean to dairy. No drainage. Water from stream Bucket Closet. Bldgs. comprise: Stone built with wood and felt roof 2 stall stable, shippen for 5 cows. Sheds. St. thatched shippen for 6 cows. Fair repair".

The family were there until at least 1936 when 'Granny' (as she was known locally) Eva died, aged 80, and is buried in Princetown Churchyard.

According to the 1851 and 1861 Census, William Williams was born in Tavistock, but in the 1871 Return he is shown as being born at Penryn in Cornwall. Joel Williams in 1861 came from Stithians, but in 1871 his birthplace was given as Penryn. Possibly William and Joel were brothers, or at least related in some way. One of my aunts married a Williams who lived in Ivy Cottage, the cottage on the north side of the Tavistock Road by The Lodge, and this Williams was the last resident, giving up the tenancy when they moved to Tavistock in 1944. The cottage was built about 1858, and as Joel is recorded as living at Rundlestone, it is very likely this was his home. It has now been renovated and is used for trekkers accommodation, comprising twelve bunk beds in three rooms.

In 1824, in the Maristow papers, John Johnson (one of the brothers who owned the railroad and the Foggintor Quarry complex) was presented to be taken Tenant for Easter Green (Yestor), also in 1825 and 1826. However, in October 1832, Giles wrote to Sir Ralph to the effect that 'Traer says Yestor is useless to Mr Johnson and therefore he is endeavouring to get someone that will cultivate it. Johnson in fact has no lease'. In February 1844, Geo. Cole, a Stone Cutter, asked if he could be allowed to remain at Yestor, but as he was a 'Tenant under Mr Johnson, his wishes cannot be complied with and therefore he must quit'. A few days later a letter was sent to Samuel Hannaford, another Stone Cutter at Princetown, to see if he 'still retained an inclination to hire Yestor'. He was advised to take a fresh look at the premises so as to see the state of the buildings and fences, in case repairs were needed. In 1845 he was presented to be taken

Ruins of Yes Tor Farm   *(Jenny Sanders)*

Ruins of Red Cottages, showing the trees which were blown down in the 1980s
(Dave Brewer)

(Elisabeth Stanbrook)

Ruins of Eva's Farm

Old buildings at Criptor Farm   *(Jenny Sanders)*

New buildings at Criptor Farm with the old buildings being to the right

(Ted Fitch)

Ivy Cottage in the snow, after being empty for many years   *(Brewer collection)*

Ivy Cottage after being refurbished in 1995/96. Now trekkers' accommodation
(Jenny Sanders)

Tenant for Easter Green and 'sworn and paid 2/6'. This could very well be the same 'Samuel Hannaford' who was presented in both 1835 and 1836 for 'removing Turf from Walkhampton Common and had no right to do so'.

There must have been a dwelling at Yestor by 1795, as in the Maristow papers a lease for an un-named tenant was mentioned, with two further leases to Joseph Spurr in the 1780s with agreements to 'rebuild' (Mike Brown). On the 1851 Census, Easter Green appears to be two 'residences', occupied by John Ponsford, his wife and two lodgers, and James Perkins with his wife and three children; in 1861 it was John Turner and wife and John Sloman, wife and three children – the occupation of Richard, the 14 year old son, was given as 'Post Boy'; by 1871 only John Sloman is mentioned, and there is no mention at all in 1881, so presumably this was when it was becoming ruinous.

George Cole was living at Fogginter by the 1851 Census, and they are shown in the middle of the Fogginter entries, the occupation being given as Stone Mason. This continued until the 1891 Census, when they appear after the Fogginter group but before West View Cottages, and 'farmer' is, for the first time, given as George's occupation. However, L. Govier in his book on *Walkhampton* says that Yellowmead Farm was the last to be founded, in about 1860, so something does not quite tie in. One son, Edwin, was also at Fogginter in the 1891 Census, and in 1903 it was agreed to let him have the tenement of Yellowmead as George had died, and of course the Cole family are still at Yellowmead Farm (now spelt Yellowmeade).

There are two other houses which are interesting, one is Criptor and the other Wheal Lucky. First, Criptor – there was a survey of the Manor of Walkhampton taken on 27 Sept Eliz (1585) by Edward Drewe, gent, in which Richard Dunynge has the tenement (1573) called Criptor with twenty acres, the rent being 6/2 and a goose (Hamilton-Leggett). 70 years are quoted but whether this is the length of the lease or time still to run is not mentioned. In 1811 a Susanna Barratt was renting Criptor; David Allen was there between 1821 and 1834 in the Conventionary Rents Book; in 1847 William Wilmot and Susanna Lewis were to be taken as tenants, and were sworn and paid 2/6d; but in 1851 we find Samuel Hannaford being sworn and paying 2/6d as tenant; by 1905 the French family were in residence. In September Mr French advised that he wished a new dwelling house and would pay an additional £10 a year rent; in April 1906 he also said he would do the haulage of materials and cut up stone for building, by May 9th the foundations were passed, June 19th the house was progressing satisfactorily, July 17th the walls were up ready for the roof, August 2nd the roof timbers were on and the work proceeding satisfactorily, by the 28th the walls were being cemented, and it was inspected on November 23rd and passed as Satisfactory. We used to go to Criptor from Foggintor for cream, but the only thing I seem to remember is a dairy with stone (granite or slate?) shelves going around the side, but childhood memories are not always to be relied upon!

Wheal Lucky Mine was first mentioned in the late 1790s, so presumably one or two cottages were soon erected nearby. In the Conventionary Rents between 1835 and 1848, Thomas Hicks was renting about four acres of 'land inclosure' near Wheal Lucky Mine, and living in one of the cottages – this is actually Thomas Hext. In 1842 a Thomas Hill (Hicks) was being presented for building a house near Stone Tor, and in both 1857 and 1858, William Hicks was being presented for building a house but 'not having the right to do so' (see Mavis Price's articles in *Dartmoor Magazine* 19 and 20 for photos of these cottages). Apparently one of the cottages was badly damaged by fire about 1900, and in 1902 C. Easterbrook (being a later member of the same family) signed an agreement for a lease for building a house. By June 1903 the house was up to the joists, in September it was being plastered, by December it was nearing completion, and in April 1904 a Certificate had been obtained from the Sanitary Inspector, and Charles Easterbrook was in possession. It also stated that 'A lease may be proposed', although nothing further was found regarding a lease, but as the family lived there until the 1970s, they presumably had one! This, of course, is the house by the roadside.

Around 1808-10 a Robert Evely was paying £2.2.0. for a 'New built house and six acres of ground adjoining Rundlestone', still being there in 1834. This was possibly the small farm at the bottom of the North Hessary track, but no further information was found.

On 4th July 1850 a letter was sent to John Perkins, 'near Granite Works', as follows: 'I understand you have been making an inclosure of some land on Sir Ralph Lopes Common of Walkhampton, and I wish you to come to my office here on Monday next in the forenoon that I may have conversation with you on the subject'. This causes a bit of a mystery, as the only 'John' appears to be an eight year old son of David Perkins of Steanlake (on the 1851 Census).

In this Census Return, Whitethorn is mentioned with the families of James Perkins and Henry Pascoe being in residence, and is entered between Easter Green (occupied by John Ponsford and James Perkins) and Criptor (occupied by Samuel Hannaford). In 1844 and 1857 we have presentments against John Perkins (again) for 'enclosing land near Whitethorn' and in 1852 the same, but to James Perkins, so maybe this is the solution to the above paragraph also.

There were also Perkins at Rundlestone Cottage on the 1861 Census and at

Mistor Lodge in 1871.

As mentioned previously, there were only two cottages at Foggintor in 1841, but Giles, on his visit to the quarries on 10th September 1841 reported that 'A great number of men were at work, about 300' working at Foggintor alone, so where did they all live? According to the 1841 Lydford Census, some of which was rather feint with quite a lot of illegible words, there were 85 occupants at the Barracks at the defunct Princetown Prison, a further 14 at the Hospital and 5 'units' nearby, with a further 23 households in Fore Street and Chapter Row. The occupants included stone masons, blacksmiths, labourers, carpenters, a millwright, farmer, grocer, baker, and 2 publicans. It is probable that some of the quarry workers came from here, as in 'The Building of Princetown Church' (*TDA* 128) Elisabeth Stanbrook states 'Although there was a mass exodus of civil and military personnel from Princetown, local people remained in some of the dwellings, and the barracks which had housed the troops were, in time, leased to the nearby quarry owners at Foggintor to accommodate their workers'. Probably some of the other quarry workers would have walked in from nearby villages, but we are still a long way off the 300 Giles saw at Foggintor. Is it possible a number travelled up on the horse-drawn wagons each day from villages on the way from Plymouth – no records to this effect have been seen but it may be the answer.

We now come to information on the first houses to be built to actually house the quarryworkers. On 30th July 1846, Giles wrote to Hoar querying why someone had left two plans for cottages with specification for building same, and on 21st August 1846 he wrote to Uren of the Granite Works to the effect that 'Sir Ralph Lopes was disposed to grant a lease for building cottages which he fully expected would be accepted by the Haytor Granite Company'. On 20th January 1847, Giles wrote to Mr Hoar:

'It was not until yesterday I could obtain any final instructions from Sir Ralph Lopes on the subject of the Proposed Cottages on Walkhampton Common near the Granite Quarry. He having on Monday morning only received the drawings of the first proposed cottages but could not judge of the improved plans you submitted to me the other day which I delayed not to lay before him. He gives the preference to the latter most decidedly supposing and requiring the cottages now proposed will be built with such materials and in the way set forth in the specification (of which I have a copy) that accompanied the former plans. I must beg to refer you to my letter of the 20th August last for particular requisitions on the part of Sir Ralph.

And as in the month of September last through Mr Filmer extension of privilege was asked that the occupiers of these cottages might be permitted to cut turf and vag on the Common for their private consumption within such cottages as ordinary household fuel but not for sale. Sir Ralph thinks 10/- (instead of 5/- as he first asked when ignorant of such requirement) should be the reserved rent for each cottage with its half acre of ground.

As to the stream of water contemplated to be brought to the cottages by a bore hole or other means and a restriction that it be applied to household purposes only and not to the working of any kind of machinery and the quantity so limited should be the minimum of the required supply Sir Ralph wishing to retain the command of water as much as possible for other purposes should it be required. Another, and to Sir Ralph, a most important stipulation is that the Haytor Granite Co. shall by the Deed which will be rendered necessary to carry into effect these arrangements for a prolonged period pledge themselves in the same manner as the Cornwall and Devon Central and Plymouth Railway and the South Devon Railway Companies have done with him in that on annoyance or trespass being committed by any of the occupiers of these Cottages or any of the labourers or other persons employed on any part of the Company's works on Sir Ralphs property and complaint thereof having been made by Sir Ralph or his known agent, the Company shall immediately thereupon be required to expel such occupier and to discharge such labourer or other person so offending.

I will take the first opportunity of sending the plan back to Mr Uren. I hope this will reach you before the assembly of the Board of Directors tomorrow and that I shall soon be favoured with a further communication from you on the subject.'

In April 1849, Giles wrote to Mr Shillibeer of Huckworthy Bridge:

'You of course know the new Cottages erected by the Haytor Granite Co. on Walkhampton Common, I believe it is a group of six with gardens. A ground plan is wanted on a small scale to be laid down on a lease now in preparation and if the elevation and section of the Cottages with their backlets could also be shewn it would be desirable. The distance from the public road from Merriville Bridge to Two Bridges should be shewn as well as the entrance road therefrom to the rear and front of the Cottages and some part of the continuation to last mentioned road towards the Quarries.

If a mile stone be near in the Merriville Road it would be well to give its bearings and distance from the Cottages or some other fixed object likely to be desirable in order to define permanently the locus in queo. I have understood all the Cottages are on the same scale and plan, therefore the section of one would do but the whole length of elevation would be necessary. I doubt not Mr Uren would on application lend assistance and probably produce the Building plan.

I shall be pleased to hear whether you can attend to this little job shortly.'

In October 1849 the Lease was sent to the London Solicitors of the Haytor Granite Co. but a few alterations had been made, and Giles wrote to them on 19th October 1849:

'Since receipt of yours of the 3rd instant, Sir Ralph Lopes has returned to Maristow, and I have consulted him respecting the alterations you have made in the draft of the proposed Lease of the Cottages, and the following is the result:

1st. The grant of cutting Turf and Vags for Fuel must be confined to some described portions of the Common and to cease upon the Commons becoming inclosed should such occur during the term.

2nd. The Water Course will be shown on the Plan but you have not yet returned the Plan.

3rd. The preservation of a pre-emption to purchase all trees and shrubs will be relinquished.

4th. Land Tax. Should any be imposed must be borne by the Lessees.

5th. Although the Road may be said to belong more strictly to the Granite Works yet as it is the only communication from the public Highway to the Cottages, that portion of it must be yielded up in good condition.

6th. The Covenant for insurance against Fire will be struck out.

7th. The proviso making void the proposed lease of the Cottages on notice from the Company of abandoning the Granite Lease must stand. In conceding to the Company the liberty of shortening the Lease of the Granite Company, and Sir Ralph considered he gave them great indulgence and in treating as to the Cottages he considered the same principles were to prevail and that the Cottages were only an appurtenant of the Granite Works. He therefore will not consent to the obliteration of the proviso.'

Although 'specifications' and 'plans' were mentioned in the Maristow papers, there only appeared to be one or two references to material used, such as on 20th August 1846 when Giles wrote to Hoar:

'.....His (Sir Ralph's) Suveyor has also looked into them and has suggested two alternatives in the specification, viz from his knowledge of the Moor he thinks Red pine sleepers on ground joists would very soon decay and recommends they should be of oak. In the next place he considers the first covering of the external framing should be rough boarding of one inch instead of half an inch thick…'

On the 20th January 1847 another letter acknowledges the drawings of the cottages and 'requiring the cottages now proposed will be built with such materials and in the way set forth in the specification'. I could find nothing regarding the actual material used in their construction, but one would assume that moorstone was used. However, I have been sent the following information which Elisabeth Stanbrook came across in the c.1913 Public Record Office records:

West View.
1.   House.
2a. 0r. 35p. 1 - 12 inclusive
Gross Value: land £3.6s. Rateable value: land £2.l0s
Occupier: Pethick Bros. Owner: Sir Henry Lopes, Bart.
Cob and timber built with slate roof house. Ground floor: 1 room. 1st floor: 1 room. Peat shed at back.
12 cottages with 6 doors, all alike 1-12 inclusive.
Bucket closet for each pair of Cotts. Water from Stream. No drainage.
Occupier: Mr Hext. 1913.

2.	As 1.	Occupier Mr Hext. 1913.
3.	As 1.	Occupier G. Mead. 1913
4.	As 1.	Occupier G. Mead. 1913
5.	As 1.	Occupier: Jm. Cooper. 1913.
6.	As 1.	Occupier: Cooper. 1913.
7.	As 1.	Occupier: R. Rich. 1913.
8.	As 1.	Occupier: Mitchell. 1913
9.	As 1.	Occupier: G. Hext. 1913
10	As 1.	Occupier: Cooper. 1913
11	As 1.	Occupier: W. Phillips 1913
12	As 1.	Occupier: J. Hannaford. 1913

With so much moorstone around, it seems strange to build these cottages with cob. Cob is usually a combination of mud/clay and straw sometimes with dung mixed in. There is also the letter Giles wrote on 20th August 1846 stating that 'the first covering of the external framing should be rough boarding 1 inch thick'. If they were built of moorstone, they would not require external wooden framing; but if they were of cob it is possible this was done to help preserve the cob against the Dartmoor weather.

Clay was found when a cutting was made for the Plymouth and Dartmoor Railway at Little King Tor in the 1820s (Burt), no doubt this would have proved suitable, although a few years later (1852) Babb of Princetown was endeavouring to make bricks from a pocket of clay found near the railway station, but this was unsuccessful.

On 27th December 1898, Giles met Mr Crowle of St Austell, at Dousland, re a Clay Sett at Princetown, but nothing further was found until June 22nd 1906, when again Giles met Mr N.N.R. Nicholls and Capt Crowe (sic) with reference to their application for a lease. This time it gives the area – 'We went over the land round Rundlestone towards Mis Tor then through the valley East of the old quarries at Foggintor and onto the other side of the Railway above Criptor. The formation of the surface indicates clay ground in each of these places and a formal application is to be made for a licence to sink trial pits...' Here again, no further reference to this was found.

At some point before 1871, the weather got into these cottages and they were covered with corrugated iron, painted with red-lead and so became known as the 'Red Cottages' by the 1871 Census. In April 1901 the condition of the buildings and cottages (which belonged to the Quarry Company) were examined, and on the 17th August Giles noted that 'Nothing has been done to woodwork and painting of Red Cottages', which is the first reference to the name 'Red Cottages' in the Maristow papers. On the 1851 Census they were referred to as Mount Pleasant, West View Cottages in 1861 and 1891, with Red Cottages in 1871 and 1881. In later years it seemed strange to call them 'Red' Cottages when they were black, having been covered with pitch – again no doubt due to the weather causing problems to the buildings.

On the 1851 Census there were eleven families living in the cottages, including my Great x 3 Grandmother with her second husband, John Ruby, and four children. Another occupant was Edward Uren, aged 27, his wife, three sons and an eleven year old General Servant, Caroline Williams from Lydford. Uren was the Superintendent of the Granite Works and was also a Local Preacher for the Bible Christians. Presumably his was the family occupying two rooms. There were 34 children, 16 lodgers and a couple of visitors, but the largest number in one room included the two parents, six children and four lodgers. How on earth did they manage!

There were only 32 Stone Masons and 12 Granite Labourers in the whole area in 1851, and apart from 21 residents at Foggintor and Red Cottages coming from Cornwall, the rest were Devonians from mainly around the moor, such as Walkhampton, Tavistock, Lydford, Chagford, Moretonhampstead, Bovey Tracey, Ashburton and Ilsington.

In 1861 at 'West View' there were fifty adults and 38 children in thirteen households, so that each of the original six cottages contained two families – on the OS map published 1906 there is what could possibly be a further building just to the north of the block which may have housed the other family, although there do not appear to be any visible ruins of such a cottage.

In 1891 a family named Moore lived at Red Cottages, including an eleven year old son called Alfred. In April 1892, Alfred 'whose parents reside at the Redstone Cottages was summoned for setting fire to Rundlestone Plantation and destroying £10 worth of young firs, the property of the prison authorities, who withdrew the charge on account of the tender age of the boy. The Chairman said if the charge had not been withdrawn, the lad would probably have been committed to the assizes, as the bench had not the power to deal with such a case' (Rendell). This extract was taken from the *Tavistock Gazette* of 1st April 1892, and is the only reference I have seen to 'Redstone Cottages'.

In the Maristow Estate Letter Book (1902-1917), is a list of Cottages 'Let to Mess (sic) Pethick with Granite Quarries' October 1905 and West View are given as follows:

Cottage No.	Occupied by:		Rent:
1 & 2.	Occupied by:	Samuel Hext.	Rent: 6.10
3 & 4		George Mead	6.10
5 & 6		Sam Cooper	6.10
7		R. Rich	3.5
8		Mrs Cooper	3.5
9		Mrs Hext	3.5
10		Mrs Cooper	3.5
11		VACANT	3.5
12		J. Hannaford	3.5

As will be seen from this, in three instances, two rooms in a cottage were let as one house, but five were still let as one room, (the sixth room being vacant), as was the case in the 1840s.

Some of the last occupiers of Red Cottages were the Cooper (2), Eden, Hext, Mead (2), Mitchell, Phillips, Rich and Shaw families.

The only reference to the cottages being built at Foggintor is on the 1851 Census where five families were mentioned as living there and TEN HOUSES BEING BUILT written across the page. William Williams was still living in the cottage he built without permission c.1841, and Robert Uren as the Superintendent of the Granite Works was presumably in the Managers' House. This leaves three families, and even though I have found no documentary evidence, I am convinced that the 'Stone Cutters Shed' mentioned in 1841 had been adapted into suitable housing, and could have housed the other three families of George Cole, William

Tremain and Joseph Udy. I always understood that the two cottages in the centre of the block had been made into one dwelling for my grandfather and his family, but as the Coles had a daughter, four sons and seven lodgers, I think it possible that they also had it as one house, with two bedrooms upstairs, a parlour and kitchen downstairs, which would be classed as two dwellings. It would definitely seem that this block was used for housing before the other ten houses in the square had been built. Opposite 'our' house was 'the backs' in which the occupants of 'our' block had small rooms for storing their wood, coal, oil for lamps, maize for the chickens, etc. I am not sure how many storage rooms there were, but I think the ten houses of the square must have had access to their rooms from their houses.

Water for the occupants of Hill Cottages was obtained from the leat, which commenced in the mire near the head of the Longash Brook just north of the Tavistock Road, and ended in a shute by the entrance to the smaller Foggintor Quarry. I have been unable to find a date for the cutting of this leat, but feel it was originally dug to feed the water-wheel. In view of the fact that Lopes wanted to retain as much water as possible 'for other purposes should it be required' would seem to imply that the water-wheel had ceased working before 1847 – it is very likely it had done so before 1841 when the Stone Masons shed was erected above the arch, although I understand it would be possible to have a water-wheel close to a building, as there are several quarries in Wales which used a similar position, such as at Ynys y Pandy and at Blaen Nantmor Quarry near Beddgelert where the wheel was situated between two large dressing sheds and extensions to the axle drove overhead line shafting within each building (Chris Stone). The occupiers of the Red Cottages were to obtain their water 'from a stream by a borehole or other means', and it is very likely this referred to a 'bullseye' stone or an 'inch hole' stone, which would restrict the water taken from the leat. These 'inch hole' stones were frequently used on Dartmoor, and are still to be seen in a number of places, such as in the leat by the Windy Post on Barn Hill not too far away. On the 1891 Census there were twelve families at Foggintor with five houses empty.

The Maristow papers also mention Hill Cottages in the Land Agents Diary:

July 27 1903.   Cottages. There have been complaints of damp walls and weak windows.

Aug. 18 1903.   Quarries. Went through cottages at Foggintor, some complaints of damp walls and wet windows.

Aug. 15 1905.   Cottages. They require some small repairs to windows, floors and plastering and painting.

Unfortunately, the outcome was not discovered.

The Maristow Letter book also gives details of Foggintor rents and occupants in October 1905, as follows:

Cottage No.		Occupied by:		Rent:	
13		VACANT			3.5
14		Samuel Stephens			5.4
15		Thomas Hext			5.4
16		Mrs (Moore)			3.5
17		Mrs Eva			3.5
18 & 19		John May			5.4
20		Sam J. Stephens			3.5
21		Joseph Ruby			5.4
22		A. Rook			3.5
23		John North			5.4
24		Wm. Perkins			5.4
25		J.Pike			3.5
26		VACANT			3.5
27	Manager's House	E.Goad			15.0

The total of the rents for West View and Foggintor was £107.19, from which was deducted Rates paid by Pethick of £10.00 and Repairs '8% of rent say' £7.19, leaving a balance of £90.

Unfortunately, we now have a problem – there were ten 'one up one down' houses built at Foggintor plus the four in 'our' block, totalling fourteen. As we see from the above, there are six families paying 5/4 – as No. 21 which was my grandfather, who had two rooms up and two down – so presumably the other five paying this rent also had the same accommodation. This adds up to twelve 'single' houses, and with the seven paying 3/5 rent, the grand total is nineteen, so where are these other houses? After referring to the archway, Albert Mead wrote in 1986 'the stables used to be the other side of the foreman's house, I can remember when they were used, a man by the name of Perkins used to be the carter in those days.' This must rule out the ruins below that house. A possibility here is that the Royal Oak bungalows had been modified for living accommodation for two families from the weighbridge (here also, nothing was found regarding this). I do feel this is very doubtful, as the weighbridge would probably still be required on site, Foggintor quarry not closing down for another year. Alternatively, they could possibly have been the 'wood built' ones mentioned below.

*Hill Cottages, taken in the late 1920s, the Chapel is the section with the wide
doorway at the right edge of the buildings, and part of the Manager's House roof
and chimney are to be seen centre left. The faint line around King Tor is the track
of the G.W.R.. (The late Albert Mead)*

Hill Cottages being demolished, 1953   *(Harry Davies)*

Ruins of Hill Cottages, taken 1996   *(Chris Stone)*

The Manager's House

(The late Ted Masson Phillips)

The ruins below the Manager's House, mentioned as being stables   (Chris Stone)

The northern houses at Hill in the snow, the Chapel is centre left
(Dave German collection)

Next we will look at the descriptions for the cottages at Foggintor which Elisabeth Stanbrook kindly sent to me after finding them in the PRO c.1913 papers:

1.   Foggintor - House.

Gross value: land £3.l0s. Rateable value: land £2.15s.

Occupier: Messrs. Pethick Bros. Owner: Sir Henry Lopes Bart

"Stone slated house in fair repair".

Ground floor: 1 room. 1st floor: 1 room.

Turf house and bucket closet for each cottage. Water from stream. No drainage.

Occupier: Stevens. 1/6 weekly inclusive. 1913.

2 & 3.   As above. One house occupied by Mrs Hext. 1913

4.   As 1. Occupier: Moore. 1913

5.   As l. Occupier: Lupe. 1913

6.   As 1. Occupier: Stevens. 1913

7.   As 1. Occupier: Down. 1913

8.   As 1. Occupier: E. Mead. 1913

9 & 10   Occupier: Ruby. One house as 2 & 3. 1913

11.   As 1. Occupier; Lloyd. 1913

12.   As l. Occupier: J. Worth. 1913

13 & 14. Occupier: Perkins. One house as 2 & 3. 1913

Other houses were also mentioned at Foggintor:

Foggintor - House

Gross value: land £2. Rateable value: land £1.l0s.

Same occupier and owner as 1.

"Wood built with wood & felt roof bungalow containing 2 rooms in good order. Peat shed,. Water from stream. No drainage. Bucket closet".

Occupier: Alf. Eva. 1/6 weekly inclusive. 1913.

Another house as above but occupied by Wilson. 1913

Two other houses as above but vacant.

Foggintor - House

Gross value: land £3.l0s. Rateable value: land £2.15s.

Same occupier & owner as 1.

"stone & slated bungalow containing 3 rooms in fair repair"

Water from stream. No drainage.

Occupier: G.C.French at 2/- inclusive. 1913

Another house as above but occupied by G.H. French. 1913

Another house as above but "stone & slated school with 3 classrooms. Used as a House once".

This causes a few problems! I had been told some years ago that there were a number of 'wooden' huts, always referred to as the 'barracks', which were still occupied after the First World War, (Albert's aunt and uncle were married then and lived there), but apart from their being near the stables and the above remarks I have no other information on them.

The 'bungalow' referred to could possibly have been the 'Royal Oak Bungalows' – one was occupied by the Youngson family, (who moved out on the Mis Tor track), and the last family to live there were called Gibbs.

I have seen in print that the Wesleyan Chapel was built in the late 1850s, but have been unable to verify this. On the OS 1885 edition it is marked as Methodist Chapel (Wesleyan) and it has also been referred to as Royal Oak Chapel. During the time it was there, apart from being used as a Chapel, where the great Billie Bray preached at times, it was also used as a school. On the 1861 Census, John Norrish living at Foggintor was given as the School Master (at 69 years of age) with 15 year old Selina Laiver as his assistant. Some time later the daughter of the foreman named Bally Gould taught there for a number of years. It was used as a Chapel and School for some years, as a private house, as a workshop for the quarry at Swell Tor (after 1906 presumably when Foggintor Quarry had closed down), later standing empty for a long time. There are one or two comments in the Maristow papers regarding the Chapel:

July 27 1903.	Foggintor Chapel. Drainage was required for two closets and permission to make a deep cesspit for the disposal of same.
Aug 18 1903.	Met Mr Mason with reference to drainage to closets. The Trustees wish to have a supply of water from the brook (leat?) for flushing out the closets and permission to make a deep cesspit for disposal of same.
24 Sept 1903.	Met Mr Mason, Sun Insurance and Trustees of Chapel about proposed cesspit. They have encroached and wish to have sufficient ground - ??? drying green at back.
Apr 4 1904.	Nothing has been done towards sanitary arrangements.

The 'drying green at back' mentioned above could possibly be behind the houses at the inner end of Big Tip, where there was a grassy area with clothes lines – not really an ideal place to put a cesspit.

The other building at Foggintor was the most important, it was the Manager's House. Referring to E. Stanbrook's notes from the Public Record Office papers again –

Foggintor

Quarries and Offices. Manager's House and labourer's cottages. 219a,2r,23p. (Covers the Foggintor houses) Gross value: £150. Rateable value: £130.

Occupier: Messrs Pethick Bros.

Owner: Sir H. Lopes, Bart, freehold.

Occupier's Tenancy Term: 21 years from 29 September 1906.

Rent: £130 first 5 years. £180 a year after.

"Granite quarries & rough moorland pasture".

This was certainly built to a much higher standard than the other houses, and the photo taken in 1932 by the late Mr E. Masson Phillips shows this, but with most of the windows boarded up. In the 11th Report of the Plymouth Branch of the Devonshire Association (1942) at Swell Tor Quarries, 'Mr R.H. Worth gave an instructive account of the geological peculiarities of the close grained and coarse grained blue and grey granites, and of the old and new methods of splitting the blocks of stone. Near the disused Royal Oak Quarries, a well-built house of granite, a former office of the quarry owners who had supplied some of the granite which was employed in the building of London Bridge was pointed out as an object lesson of what could be achieved with that type of rock'. The house also had a walled garden attached, with fruit trees and vegetables, outside of which was a small pond with ducks. Could this have been the 'substantially built Cottage' mentioned by Giles on his visit on 10th September 1841?

In 1895, as there were about 60 children in the area receiving no schooling, the Dartmoor Mission Hall for undenominational worship, which was built in 1887 at Rundlestone, was brought into use as a school, at a rent of £5 per annum, so the quarry school was by then closed. Under the 1902 Education Act, a Board of Managers was established, and were responsible to the newly formed County Education Authority. The Mission Hall building was considered unsuitable and there were doubts that the Hall could legally be used as a school, so Foggintor Chapel was again brought into use as the school.

On the 1891 Census, the occupants of the Mission Room are given as Joseph

Collins, aged 46, a Civil Guard from Maker, with his wife, Elizabeth, their four children, Lillie Richards an adopted daughter aged 6 and Lillie Rook aged 14 a Servant both from Lydford. Elisabeth Stanbrook sent me details from the Public Record Office c.1913 papers as follows:

Mission Hall, Foggintor

House

Gross value: land £8.15s. Rateable value: £7

Occupier: W. Rich

Owner: W. Rich. Foggintor, Nr Princetown. Freehold. Invested in Trustee.

Occupier's Tenancy Term: monthly

Rent: £7.10s.

"Stone & plastered house with slate roof in good order". Ground Floor: 2 Rooms, lean to stone and corrugated iron roof wash house, lean to stone and corrugated iron roof shed to end of house. 1st Floor: 3 Rooms.

Water. Spring laid on to yard. Drainage to moor. 3 stone and corrugated iron roof closets at back. Large stone and slated Mission Hall to hold about 100, adjoining house match boarded inside.

The last occupants were Tom Hext and his family, and it was finally closed in 1940. Apparently American soldiers stationed at nearby Foggintor during the war were the last people to use the chapel. For 27 years the chapel stood unused, and Miss Kathleen Hext moved out in December 1966, after her Father's earlier death. Miss Hext said she did not think the chapel should be pulled down, as it was a part of Dartmoor, but a spokesman for the Maristow Estate, the owners, said:

'The National Park committee have always wanted to pull it down. It was in a deplorable condition and was no use to anyone.' (*Tavistock Times* 18th August 1967).

A school was definitely needed in the area, and after a lot of problems, Walkhampton Foggintor School was started in 1914. West Mead Quarry was possibly working and building stone from there used, also no doubt from Merrivale Quarry and Hollow Tor Quarry. It was opened on April 19th 1915 under Mr F.S. Stoyle, who was the only schoolmaster there during the school's life, and took pupils from the Foggintor, Rundlestone and Merrivale areas. The photograph of the school shows Mr Stoyle's house just behind to the right. The two buildings nearest the road were the separate boys' and girls' entrances, with cloakrooms and toilets, the main building containing two classrooms, one for infants and one for 11 to 14-year-olds, hall, etc. The buildings were very substantially built, having wood block floors with solid fuel (coke) central heating. Most of the pupils took

(Brewer Collection)

Walkhampton Foggintor School

Probably the last photo taken of the pupils at Walkhampton Foggintor School, in 1935   *(Brewer collection)*

Sid Warren, Pauline Warne, Dorothy Jeffery, Betty Shaw, Ed. Jeffery
Eric Green, Ivy Gibbs, Doreen Maddocks, Jane Ellacott, Dennis Martin
K. Gibbs, Kevin Ellacott, Donald Warne, Alex Shaw, Gerald Rich, Jack Sarjeant,
Gerald Green.

The Mission Hall, Rundlestone.   *(Ron Joy collection)*

The houses on the Mis Tor Track, Rundlestone   *(Brewer collection)*

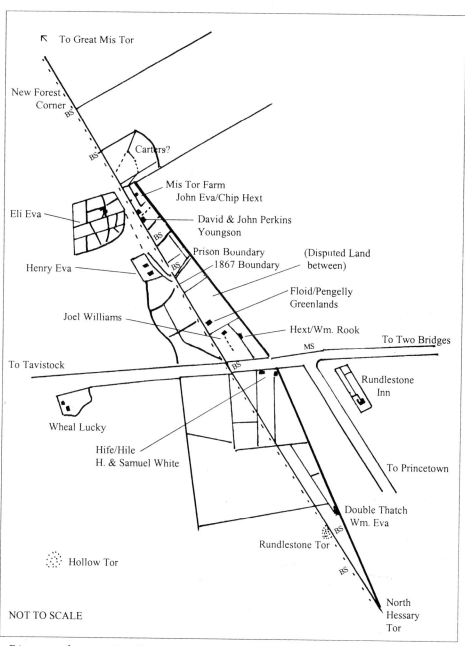

To Great Mis Tor

New Forest Corner
BS

Carters?
BS

Mis Tor Farm
John Eva/Chip Hext

Eli Eva

David & John Perkins
Youngson
BS

Prison Boundary
1867 Boundary
BS

(Disputed Land
between)

Henry Eva

Floid/Pengelly
Greenlands

Joel Williams

Hext/Wm. Rook

MS
To Two Bridges

To Tavistock
BS

Rundlestone
Inn

Wheal Lucky

Hife/Hile
H. & Samuel White

To Princetown

Double Thatch
Wm. Eva
BS

Rundlestone Tor

BS

Hollow Tor

North
Hessary
Tor

NOT TO SCALE

Diagram showing Rundlestone Cottages and the disputed Forest/Walkhampton
Manor boundary

pasties for their mid-day meal, which were heated on the pipes, or later in a double burner oil stove. The school bell was very prominent on the roof of the main building. Behind the school buildings were the separate boys' and girls' playgrounds, with the house and garden behind the boys' playground, and the coke store and playing field behind the girls'. There were pupils at this school until its closure in 1936, when they had to transfer to Princetown School (which was founded in 1862). The buildings were left empty for some time, and in 1938 the property was bought by a Dr Adamson who lived there for a time – I think he must have named it 'Four Winds' which is the name the National Park car park, which was resurfaced and enlarged in 1981, continues to be known by. When he left various plans arose, to turn it into a restaurant or petrol station, but nothing materialised, and according to the *Western Morning News* of 2nd March 1964, 'at a public enquiry last June, it was described as a 'grave disfigurement' in a stretch of completely open moorland'. It was demolished in February/March 1964 by ten boys, aged between 16 and 18, from the Northbrook Approved School, under the care of two masters at the school, both building instructors, Mr G.W.N. Ricketts and Mr G. Buxton. The work took about a month, and the rubble was used on the construction of the new section of road at Devil's Elbow on the Princetown/Yelverton road. However, the two-storey house adjacent to the school was left at that time, and demolished by other boys from Northbrook in a similar exercise the following year.

It has been a bit of a problem trying to decide where most of the houses at Rundlestone were, as the various Census Returns put them all under Rundlestone, Mount Pleasant or Mount View at different times, but I think they are as follows:

Double Thatch Cottage (on east of North Hessary track)

1861-81	William Eva

Two buildings (on west of Mis Tor track by main road)

1861	Hile and Hife

1881 Henry and Samuel White (name marked on 1881 O.S. map in ink)

North side of road.

House on east:	1861	John Hext
	1871	Hugh Hill
	1881 and 1891	William Rook
House on west:	1861	Joel Williams (later known as Ivy Cottage and occupied by same family to 1944)

Mis Tor Track:

First on East side:	1861	Richard Floid. (Greenlands - this is the only mention of this name)
	1881	Pengelly (written on 1881 O.S. in ink)
First West side:	1861 & 1871	Henry Eva
	1871 & 1881	Ann Floyd
	1881	Jane Eva (Henry's widow)
Second East side:	1861	Rundlestone Cottage. David Perkins
	1871	Rundlestone Lodge. David Perkins
	1881	John Perkins (family there until 1930s)
Last East side:	1861	John Eva
	1881	Elizabeth Eva (John's widow)
		Mistor. William Eva
	1891	Henry Eva
Last West side:	1881	Eli Eva (son of Richard)
		Richard Eva
	1891	Eli Eva
		Honor Eva (widow of Richard)

I understand there were three farms and two smallholdings on the Mis Tor track. In 1861 John Eva was farming forty acres, but in 1871 only four; in 1881 his widow was farming ten acres, and his son William six acres; 1871 showed Henry Eva farming six acres, Ann Floyd just two and David Perkins ten acres.

Some time in the past I was told verbally that two families from Foggintor, by the name of Perkins (John?) and Rook (William?), moved to Rundlestone 'some years ago', one putting an 'X' for his signature and getting a 40 year lease, whereas the other could read and refused to sign until he had a 99 year lease. Naturally, I do not know whether there is any truth in this story or which person did what!

The names I have of the last occupiers of the properties on the Mis Tor track are Pengelly, Youngson and Chip Hext on the east side with the Eva family still being at the lower property on the West side.

J.Ll.W. Page in 1895 gave his observations of the Rundlestone area in *An Exploration of Dartmoor*:

'What the Rundlestone may have been I know not, nor could I ever ascertain; * (A tall stone stands by a gate in the wall near the turning to Princetown. It is inscribed with a raised R. This may be the Rundlestone, but no one in the neighbourhood could tell me what it signified) but the hamlet now bearing the name consists of a few scattered cottages which, as they approach Mis Tor, become somewhat poverty-stricken in appearance.

The whitewashed walls are low and sturdy, as walls on Dartmoor must needs be, the ragged thatch is often held in place by ropes of straw or hemp, and not unfrequently weighted with stone as well. Ideas of cleanliness do not prevail among these cottars, and the space round the door would, were it not for the strong Moor breeze, be redolent of ancient vegetable and soapsuds. But look at the children. Unkempt, unwashed, their hair bleached by the sun, they are as rosy, sturdy specimens of humanity as you will see between John O'Groats and Lands End. Sumptuous fare is not theirs; bacon and cabbage, I fancy, form the staple of their rough-and-ready dinner, but Dartmoor air does the rest. Go where you will on these highlands, you will find the rising generation the same generally dirty, mostly hatless, but pallid never'.

With so many Dartmoor dwellers living to ripe old age, it must definitely be something to do with the 'Dartmoor air' as Page says.

Some of the names mentioned more than once in the Census Returns include: Cole, Duke, Easterbrook, Eva, Floyd, Hext, Pascoe, Perkins, Ruby, Sloman, Stephens, Udy, Uren, White and Williams, with a few of the families, including different generations, staying for some time, some moving from Red Cottages to Foggintor and vice versa. Latterly the names included Bailey, Cooper, French, Green, Maddock, Mead, Rich, Stephens and Worth. The cottages mentioned were occupied for many years, some longer than others, and some laying empty for periods at a time. The unoccupied Hill Cottages were repaired and about six Plymouth blitz families moved there, including one family related to some of the local families, the mother having been born in the old Chapel in 1900 when it was in use as a house. Most people had moved away by the late 1940s, although one family was still in occupation at Hill Cottages at the time of the 1951 Census. Hill Cottages were demolished in 1953, and it is very probable that Red Cottages were demolished around the same time, also some of the ones at Rundlestone. My cousins helped with the demolition of Hill Cottages, and the rubble from there was used to erect the building on North Hessary Tor under the television mast.

SOME REMINISCENCES

I have always loved the area, and couldn't wait to go out there for holidays - I always felt I was going 'home'. We usually went by train to Plymouth, and via Yelverton to King Tor Halt. In summer we were more likely to go by train, or occasionally by bus, to Moretonhampstead, and then across the moor by bus to

Princetown. My first memory is being taken by train from King Tor Halt to Burrator Halt, when I could not have been more than three or four, and thinking what a beautiful place it was. It is not so easy to feel that way these days with so many wire fences and stiles all over the place, which I am sure are quite unnecessary. When going shopping to Bolt's Store in Princetown, if we did not go on the train, we would either walk out to the Mission Hall and follow the road around, or, more likely, follow the Tavistock/Ashburton track under North Hessary Tor. A van went from Bolt's Store twice a week to Foggintor, with 'everything' on board, particularly a good selection of sweets for the children. It was a marvellous area for playing, but we were not allowed in the larger quarry, nor to the west of Yellowmead farm due to the boggy area around that branch of the Longash Brook. Hemery, in *High Dartmoor* refers to the ' Pila Brook', but on mentioning this name to a cousin who had lived at Foggintor until her marriage, she said she had never heard of it and I was informed in no uncertain terms that it was the Longash Brook! Big Tip was a favourite place, but I am very sad to see all the erosion on both sides in recent years due to climbers who have left their stakes hammered on to the top, as is also the case around the rim of the larger quarry. I know also that it sounds rather silly, but I can only remember nice weather - plenty of sunshine or snow, but definitely no rain: I have of course been told of atrocious weather there, torrential rain, blizzards when one had to stay indoors, and very strong winds when it was virtually impossible to leave the shelter of the house walls because of the probability of being blown over.

Several films were shot in the area, I think one was 'The Hound of the Baskervilles', probably about 1935/36. My informant told me that a car chase was included, and he helped build a ramp above the quarry for the car to go over the top. As there was only one shot possible, numerous cameras were placed strategically, with a dummy in the car for the final fall. The Duchy Hotel, where the cast were staying, sent out a lorry daily with food for the stars and crew, who ate off trestle tables covered with white tablecloths. The Scottish actor Will Fyffe, was in another film 'Owd Bob', and when filming was completed, he gave Gran the shepherd's crook he used in the film. Unfortunately, I never saw the film, but on talking to someone in Princetown (not a resident) a few years ago, it was the first film he had ever seen.

Many years ago the occupants at Hill Cottages used to cut peat for their fires. There are no prominent ties visible, but it was cut, on Saturdays, by all the occupants of the cottages, below the south east side of Big Tip outside the field walls and going towards King Tor. Some of the peat cuttings were 'double' which meant that two cuts deep were taken along the tie. Two slabs of peat were stood up as an inverted 'V' with a third placed on top, and then left to dry. The slabs were then placed in 'stooks' with a large slate or stone on the top, which would keep them dry, apart from the side pieces, until needed within the next twelve months or so. Peat was also cut near the Longash Brook below Foggintor School by W. Cornish of Merrivale, but I am not sure where the occupants of Red Cottages obtained theirs – probably also in the Longash Brook area. Pasties were at their best when cooked on an iron griddle with hot peat stacked over and around them!

Quarrymen's funerals were quite an event. The men would wear white trousers, black waistcoats, white gloves and bowler hats. They would march along in a double column, often up to 200 men attending. At intervals, the first six men stepped aside until the coffin, at the rear of the line, reached them, they would then take the coffin from the bearers, and march along again at the rear of the line, this being repeated until the churchyard was reached. When wheeled vehicles arrived, the 'older' generation did not like it, as they thought it was undignified to get the coffin to the church at such speed. I have been told that when my grandfather was killed at Swell Tor his eldest son and the next door neighbour made the coffin in the storeroom in the backs.

There was a White Witch living locally, and when one of the men cut his arm badly with a scythe whilst cutting rushes at Snakey Bottom for thatching hayricks and the bleeding could not be stopped, he was taken to the cottage. I am told the occupant quoted some passages from the Bible, and miraculously the bleeding stopped. This person could also remove warts.

I had the following true story from the person involved, who unfortunately died a few years ago well into his seventies. He was bitten by an adder near the Longash Brook, walked a quarter of a mile back to the school, where Mr Stoyle tried to suck the poison out. The lad was then carried home to Hill Cottages, but the poison spread, and his leg started turning black from the foot upwards. It was a well-known fact that if you were bitten by an adder, that particular adder must be killed to ensure that the victim survives. The men went looking for the adder at the spot the boy mentioned to them, and a couple of days later one was killed there. Strange as it may seem, the poison immediately started receding on the death of the adder with no ill effects afterwards to the victim!

The occupants of Red Cottages were very proud of their front steps, and it was a notable feature of the block that the granite steps were scrubbed until they were literally white, and woebetide anyone who then trod on the steps! There were often lines of beautiful white sheets, pillowcases, tablecloths and towels on the clothes lines at both Hill and Red Cottages, the ladies from the latter cottages also doing the washing for the Two Bridges Hotel. One of my aunts used to walk to Princetown and spend the day at the Duchy Hotel washing clothes, and then more often than not walked home again. I have recollections of hearing she got paid 2/6d for this – 12½p in today's currency.

It has been recorded elsewhere (Crossing for one), that whortleberries ('urts) were picked and taken to various Markets. One of my cousins recalls that as a lad he helped pick them on the moor between the track and North Hessary Tor, and then carried them in a bath tub to Tavistock, where they were bought for 2d a pint. In those days the locals used to swale the moor there to encourage the growth of the whortleberries. They are certainly not so plentiful in that area these days.

We had a very prolific vegetable garden in the walled plot between the end cottage and the lane; our washing line was out on 'the green' on Big Tip, where the chickens also had free range. The houses at Hill were one room upstairs and one room downstairs – we had two rooms up and two rooms down, which was classed as two houses. This was certainly better than the occupants of Red Cottages when first built, only having one room per family. The kitchen had a large black-leaded grate with ovens, with a settle to help keep the draught out. The parlour was kept for the men-folk on Saturday evenings to enjoy their pint. I imagine bath nights must have been a problem, as the zinc bath had to be placed in front of the fire and filled with hot water. After writing that, I am now a bit curious as to where and how it was emptied!

There is one other building which could be mentioned – it was not built on Walkhampton Common, but was within the Forest of Dartmoor. It was a public house called Rundlestone Inn, supposedly built in the 1830s for the quarry workers in the area (Paul Rendell) being at the junction of the Princetown/Two Bridges Road. The Lydford Census of 1841 gives Hugh Hill, aged 56, as the publican; it closed in 1854 when a replacement, the Prince of Wales Inn in Princetown, was built. There were two Hugh Hills living at Blackabrook in 1861, Hugh of the Inn was 74 and a farmer, whilst the other Hugh (son?) was 53 and his occupation was given as a Stoker at the Princetown Gasworks. In 1871 Hugh Snr. was back in Rundlestone and still farming.

Previously I said I could not find out why Foggintor Quarries and Cottages were called 'Hill'. Someone recently suggested that as Hugh Hill was a publican and farmer and presumably fairly wealthy, was it possible he had some connection with the cottages and the quarry? Of course there is no evidence that this is so and only a slim outside chance that there is any likelihood that it is feasible. Here again there is a conflict with the spelling of Rundlestone, the Census refer to Rundlestone, whereas the Duchy refer to Rendlestone. Sale details in February 1882 showed that the Inn had over 26 acres of land, which included Church Park Dwelling House and two fields called Rock Park and West of the Leat (the Prison leat). All that now can be seen of the inn is a level piece of ground where it once stood.

It really is surprising how much was crammed into such a short period of time – the railways lasting under 140 years, the quarries a few years longer – it would be wonderful to be able to go back in time and see the tors in their original magnificence before they were so badly destroyed – and the houses only lasting a fraction over a hundred years. There is no getting away from it, this is all part and parcel of the Moor's History, which makes it all the more intriguing in trying to unravel its past as accurately as possible.

THE LOPES FAMILY AND MARISTOW PAPERS

There have been numerous references to the Maristow papers (the remainder of which were deposited at the West Devon Record Office in Plymouth some years ago after a bad fire at Maristow), and the Lopes family, so a few comments may help.

Manasseh Massey Lopes was born in Jamaica in 1755, an only son of an old Jamaican family of Spanish Jews, who inherited his father's large fortune. He bought the estate of the late James Modyford Heywood in 1798, which comprised the Manors of Maristow, Buckland Monachorum, Walkhampton, Shaugh Prior and Bickleigh, and in 1808 he acquired the Manor of Meavy. Altogether he had about 32,000 acres, which included all the land, the quarries, cottages and most of the railway was on. In 1805 he acquired a baronetcy; he was a Member of Parliament in the House of Commons in several parliaments, and was a Magistrate and Deputy Lieutenant of Devon, also High Sheriff of the County in 1810 and Lt. Col. Commandant of the Roborough Volunteers. He died at Maristow on 26th March 1831 leaving a great fortune estimated at £800, 000. He is buried in a vault at Bickleigh Church, where there is also a marble memorial to him.

In both the Maristow papers and comments by Burt, Sir Manaseh was often referred to as Sir Masseh.

His baronetcy passed to Ralph Franco, son of his sister Esther, on the condition that he changed his name to Lopes. He was born on 10th September 1788 and died on 26th January 1854, there being a massive wall memorial to him in Bickleigh Church. Sir Ralph also served in several parliaments, was a Magistrate and Deputy Lieutenant of Devon, also a Deputy Warden of the Stannaries. (*Old Devon*, Hoskins for both Sir Manasseh and Sir Ralph)

Sir Ralph was succeeded by his son, Massey, who was born on 14th June 1818 and died on 20th January 1908. There is a brass plaque in Bickleigh Church, and a similar one at Walkhampton.

(*Heraldic & Genealogical Notes from Dartmoor Churches* by Mike Brown for all three members of the Lopes family)

Sir Massey was succeeded by Henry, presumably his son, in 1908, but unfortunately I have no information on him.

As for Maristow itself, a careful restoration and conversion of the listed house and estate buildings was undertaken in 1996; some of the houses have been sold, but one or two are still available (*Western Morning News* 25.1.1997)

The other very involved person in all the events was George Giles, who was born in 1788, and was the Steward of the Maristow Estate for nearly fifty years from 1810, being very much the right-hand man of Sir Ralph. Unfortunately nothing much seems to have been discovered about the rest of his life, apart from his being buried in a large chest tomb in Bickleigh Graveyard. (Brown)

George Giles wrote numerous letters from his office at Jump (the old name for Roborough) to F.W. Filmer who worked for the Johnson Granite Company at Plymouth, and I.C.D. Hoar who was with the Haytor Granite Company at Westminster.

It would appear that there were numerous problems with the Johnsons over the years, and the following quotes, from the Maristow Estate Letter Books, throw some light on them, even though they are not strictly within the area covered.

21. 7.1838. Sir Ralph desires at the next renewal of the Licence for Maristow Inn, Doustiland, (Dousland) that the name be changed to 'The Manor Inn'.

26. 4.1842. Last year of Johnsons tenancy at Doustiland, Inn must be put back in good order, including repairs to building.

19. 8.1842. Giles visited the inn at Doustiland - never witnessed any premises in such a shocking state; approaching ruin, land overrun with thistles, docks, etc.

22. 5.1843. Requesting rent up to Christmas.

22. 6.1843. Requesting settlement.

19. 9.1843. To Filmer. Saw advertisement for sale of Hay and Corn at Doustiland. Lease requires it to be left on premises.

23.10.1843. State of Doustiland Estate - repairs required, land cleared. Sir Ralphs Surveyor reckons £137.15.9 due; repairs left to be done another £66.8.2. Both surveyors should meet there and discuss it.

30. 4.1844. Johnson. Requesting rent, and repair to dilapidation at Doustiland.

21.	5.1844.	Rent still due.	
6.	7.1844.	Very overdue bill for rent	£140.0.0.
		Lime Kiln, Stables and Laira Bridge	35.0.0.
		Small Tithe for Wharf Field	10.6.
		Dilapidations at Yestor	17.19.6
			£193.10.0

27. 6.1845. Johnson. Rents and Dilapidations at Yestor due.

20. 8.1845. Sir Ralph. Happy at last to report receipt of Johnsons Rent, £300.

16.10.1845. Hoar. Haytor Granite Co,. Rent due.

23. 5.1846. Hoar. Haytor Granite Co. Rent £83.19.0 due.

18. 4.1854. Johnson, Westminster.

'As by your favour of the 23rd December last, I understand you had disposed of your interest in the late Railway Line and the Marsh land of the South Devon Railway Company from Lady Day preceeding I waited until a years rent was due on the 25th ulto when I applied to Mr Whiteford, the Solicitor of the South Devon Co. for it. I have just received his reply to this effect, that the Company have only purchased from Christmas last, to which period you have to pay the rent (and the fees?) subsequently. I therefore have to request your remittance for the three-quarters as per annexed account.'

In a similar vein, Kendall mentions the year 1877 and a few sentences further on says:

'Another interesting sideline lies in the surrender of the lease of the Rock Hotel at Yelverton to Sir Massey Lopes in return for the latter giving up all claims in respect of dilapidations (this "man of property" aspect of the Plymouth and Dartmoor was not mentioned in any other place in the minutes, so it is difficult to say when the lease was taken up: it would, however, go some way toward explaining why the Rock Hotel was favoured with a private siding constructed of granite 'rails').'

This raises the question - was it the Johnsons who had originally taken a lease on The Rock Hotel and left it with dilapidations as they did at Doustiland and Yes Tor?

I am indebted to Mike Brown for sending me the following information he has just come across in the 1833-1858 Maristow Stewards' Accounts, and I have included his comments:

26.3.1833 John Johnson recd for Rents dues &c to Xmas last, viz

12m Rent of Doustiland & Lake	£65 0s 0d
12m do. of Yestor	£18 0s 0d
12m do. House at Horrapit	£3 0s 0d
Great Tithes of Doustiland, Lake & Yestor	£3 3s 6d
12m Rent Lime kilns Lary (Laira) Bridge	£25 0s 0d
12m do Stables &c do.	£10 0s 0d
12m do. Railway Inn do.	£12 0s 0d
12m do. Marsh Land	£10 0s 0d
8374 tons 6ft of Granite from Walkhampton Commons @ 2d	£69 15s 8d
Bog Earth & Granite Spalls	£1 8s 0d

This and the next entry were the only ones which recorded the amount of granite raised in amongst the rents:

8.3.1834 3079 tons 6ft of Granite · £25 13s 0d

The actual Property Rents remained the same as listed above for years but after 1834 the format of recording changed, and included amongst the Rental entries are the following:

10.3.1835 North Devon Wharf & Dues on Granite £100

4.5.1836 John & William Johnson...their Rents in Walkhampton are credited in the Rentals of this Manor

3.5.1837 (as above)

This note was recorded also in the 1838 and 1839 Accounts when it reverted to the same words as used in 1835:

8.7.1840 Granite Dues & North Devon Wharf £100

This remained the same in 1841 and 1842, and my interpretation is that the Johnsons must have agreed to pay a fixed sum for granite raised after 1834, which would explain not only why the sum remained exactly the same year to year, but also why it was no longer necessary for the Maristow Steward to record the tonnage.

In 1843 the sum for dues/rent increased; the following is the complete transcript from this year:

5.7.1843 ...Doustiland & Lake	£65 0s 0d
...Yestor	£18 0s 0d

Granite Dues & North Devon Wharf	£140	0s 0d
...House at Horrapit	£3	0s 0d
...Lime Kilns Stables &c Lary Bridge	£35	0s 0d
...Railway Inn	£12	0s 0d
...Marsh Land	£10	0s 0d
...Rail Road to Lime Kilns		2s 6d

Rent Charge in Lieu of Great Tithes Doustiland &c £1 16s 10½d

The entries then continue more or less in this format for a few years, but with the following differences (note also that the payments are getting more and more in arrears, being paid on a later date almost every year!):

12.8.1844	9m Rent Doustiland & Lake to Michas. 1843 when they quitted	£48	15s 0d
	Dilapidations of Doustiland & Lake when quitted, as compromised	£150	0s 0d

In 1845 the Haytor Granite Co first appears in the Rentals, but still paid the Rents on the Railway Inn etc at Laira in their own name right up to 1858:

13.8.1845	The Haytor Granite Company recd for 12m Rents due at Xmas last, viz.		
	North Devon Wharf & Granite Dues	£140	0s 0d
	Lime Kilns & Stables Lary Bridge	£35	0s 0d
Aug.16	J & W Johnson recd Rents as under, viz.		
	3m for Yestor due Lady day 1844	£4	10s 0d
	12m Rent Railway Inn to Xmas 1844	£12	0s 0d
	12m Rent Marsh Land at do.	£10	0s 0d
	12m acknowledgment for Rail road at Lairy Bridge		2s 6d
	Recd for the dilapidations of Yestor at the time they quitted Lady day 1844	£17	19s 10d
1.6.1846	J & W Johnson recd 15m Rent of the Railway Inn & Marsh Land at Lairy due Lady day last	£27	10s 0d
Nov 6	J & W Johnson 6m Rent on Railway Inn and Marsh Land near Lairy Bridge due Michas. last	£11	0s 0d
Nov.14	Haytor Granite Company recd 6m Rent due Michas. last viz. Granite Dues & North Devon Wharf	£70	0s 0d
	Lime Kilns Stables &c Lairy Bridge	£17	10s 0d
17.5.1847	J & W Johnson..6m Rent of Railway Inn...(etc)...	£11	0s 0d
June 7	Haytor Granite Company...		
	Granite Dues..(etc)	£95	0s 0d
	Lime Kilns ...(etc)...	£17	10s 0d

Dec 17	J & W Johnson...Railway Inn...	£11 0s 0d

Entries are recorded in this format until the end of the ledgers, the last entry being in 1858, continuing to be split between J & W Johnson (Railway Inn, etc) and Haytor Granite Co. (Dues, Lime Kilns, etc). From 1851 onwards the following entry is added to the Haytor Granite Company Rents (the sum is the bi-annual Rent, paid every six months):

23.6.1852	Six cottages Walkhampton Common	15s 0d

In the following year the form of words used was slightly different:

12.7.1853	Six cottages near the Quarries	15s 0d

(This must refer to the Red Cottages, where there were six. KB)

From all the preceeding information, it would appear that in spite of Sir Thomas Tyrwhitt's 'dream' and the involvement of important subscribers, the only people to really get any financial gain from the whole enterprise must have been the Johnson Brothers, with their taking control of the railway and quarries so early in the proceedings, and probably to a lesser degree, the Lopes family for numerous ground rents.

Whatever happened, it was the end of an interesting era.

BIBLIOGRAPHY

Bastin. Colin Henry.	*Princetown Railways,* 1989.
Bray, Mrs A.E.	*The Borders of the Tamar & Tavy.* 3 volumes. 1838
Brewer, Dave.	*Boundary Markers around Dartmoor,* unpublished edition.
Brown, Mike.	Notes compiled from the Maristow Papers Stewards' Accounts 1833-1858, Reference 874/3 at the West Devon Record Office, Plymouth. *Heraldic & Geneaological Notes from Dartmoor Churches. Gleanings from Parish Registers, Volume 1.*
Burt, W.	Preface and Notes in Carrington N.T., *Dartmoor, a Descriptive Poem,* 1826.
Crossing, W.	*Guide to Dartmoor,* 1970 Edition. David & Charles. *Dartmoor Worker.* David & Charles 1966. *One Hundred Years on Dartmoor.* Western Morning News 1901.
Dilley, John.	The High Moor Railway. *The Devon Historian* No. 37. October 1988
Evans, Rachel.	*Home Scenes of Tavistock and its Vicinity.* 1846.
Ewans, M.C.	*The Haytor Granite Tramway & Stover Canal.* David and Charles 1977
Gill, Crispin.	*Plymouth, A New History.* Devon Books 1993.
Gover,Mawer & Stenton.	*The Place Names of Devon,* Cambridge University Press, Part 1,1931.
Govier, L.	*Walkhampton, the Story of a Parish.* 1984
Hamilton-Leggett, P.R.	*The Manor of Walkhampton 1585.* Walkhampton Local History Publications No. 1.
Hemery, Eric.	*Walking the Dartmoor Railroads.* David & Charles 1983. *High Dartmoor.* Hale 1983
Hoskins, W.G.	*Old Devon.* David and Charles 1966
Johnson, William.	On the Quarries of Dartmoor and their Railways and Machinery. *British Association for the Advancement of Science* Part II 1841
Kendall, H.G.	*The Plymouth & Dartmoor Railway.* Oakwood Press 1968
Kingdom, Anthony R..	*The Princetown Branch.* Oxford Publishing 1979

Maristow Papers, WDRO Plymouth. Court Leet. 874/42 1811-36
874/43 1837-58
874/39 1869-87
Estate Agents Diary 874/23/1
Estate Letter Books 874
Conventionary Rents 874/19/1 1811-20
874/19/2 1821-34
874/19/3 1835-45

Page, J.Ll.W. *An Exploration of Dartmoor.* Seeley & Co. 1895

Rhodes, A.J. *Dartmoor Prison 1806-1932.* The Bodley Head. 1933

Roche, T. W. E. *Go Great Western, Reminiscences of the G. W. R. Main Line and Branches in Devon.* 1966.

Somers Cocks *Devon & Cornwall Notes & Queries.* 1971 Part 1, XXXII. (D&C N&Q) *The Haytor Granite Quarries.*

Stanbrook,Elisabeth. Notes compiled at the Public Record Office from IR58/66 527; IR58/66 528; Plymouth & Dartmoor Railway Minute Book.

Stanier, Dr. P. *Quarries and Quarrying.* Shire Publication 1985. The Granite Quarrying Industry in Devon & Cornwall Part 1 & 2 in *Industrial Archaeology Review*, VII 2 Spring 1985 & IX I Autumn 1986. Granite Quarry Cranes of Cornwall & Devon: Vanishing Industrial Archaeology. *Journal of the Trevithick Society.* The London Bridge Widening. *Stone Trades Journal* January 1904.

Stuart, W. *Prospectus of the Plymouth and Dartmoor Rail Road.* 8.1.1819.

Thomson,Sir Basil H. *The Story of Dartmoor Prison.* Heinemann 1907

Transactions of the Devonshire Association. (T.D.A.)
37 (1905) Sir Thomas Tyrwhitt. Brooking Rowe.
74 (1942) Report of Plymouth Branch. R.H. Worth
128 (1996) Building of Princetown Church Elisabeth Stanbrook

Tyrwhitt Sir T.   *Substance of a Statement made to the Chamber of*
                         Commerce concerning the Formation of a Rail Road
                         From the Forest of Dartmoor to the Plymouth Lime
                         Quarries. 3.1.1818.
Worth. R. Hansford.   *Dartmoor.* 1953
Various Newspapers
                         Mining Journal, 5, 1842.
                         Plymouth and Devonport Weekly Journal. 29.10.1840.
                         Tavistock Times 1.4.1892, 18.8.1967.
                         Western Morning News, 2.3.1964, 6.12.1995, 28.10.1996,
                         25.1.1997.

FURTHER READING, articles from *Dartmoor Magazine*:
  4 Autumn 1986.   Old Lady of the Moor. Barbara Stevens
  4 Autumn 1986.   The G.W.R.on Dartmoor. R.Chorley
  6 Spring 1987.   The Foggintor Area Part 1. Kath Brewer
  7 Autumn 1987.   The Foggintor Area Part 2. Kath Brewer
  8 Autumn 1987.   Walking the Merrivale Light Railway. John Robins
 12 Autumn 1988   School in the Middle of Nowhere. Barbara Stevens
 14 Spring 1989.   Memories of Life at Foggintor School House. Freddie
                      Stoyle
 15 Summer 1989   Sir Thomas Tyrwhitt. Les Landon
 19 Summer 1990   Two Old Ladies of the Moor. Part 1 Mavis Price
 20 Autumn 1990   Two Old Ladies of the Moor. Part 2 Mavis Price
 20 Autumn 1990   Clay Workings on Walkhampton Common. P. Rendell
 22 Spring 1991   Great Blizzard of 1891. Blaze Redgrave
 23 Summer 1991   The Foggintor Cottages. Kath Brewer
 25 Winter 1991   Walkhampton, A Brief History of a Dartmoor Parish.
                      P.Hamilton-Leggett
 42 Spring 1996   The Story of Charles & Charlotte Easterbrook.
                      Mavis Price
Stanbrook, Mary   *Old Dartmoor Schools Remembered.* Quay
                      Publications, Brixham. 1991.

INDEX